The Ultimate Quiz Book

cosmogirl

THE ULTIMATE Quiz Book

Discover the Real You!

From the Editors of CosmoGIRL

HEARST BOOKS

A division of Sterling Publishing Co., Inc.

New York / London

www.sterlingpublishing.com

Quizzes in this book were compiled from the following
previously published titles:
CosmoGirl Quiz Book: All About Guys;
CosmoGirl Quiz Book: All About You;
CosmoGirl Quiz Book: Discover Your Personality;
CosmoGirl Quiz Book: Discover Your Secret Self; and
CosmoGirl Quiz Book: Discover Your Style.

10 9 8 7 6 5 4 3 2 1

Published by Hearst Books
A division of Sterling Publishing Co., Inc.
387 Park Avenue South, New York, NY 10016

CosmoGIRL and Hearst Books are trademarks
of Hearst Communications, Inc.

www.cosmogirl.com

For information about custom editions, special sales, premium and corpo-
rate purchases, please contact Sterling Special Sales Department
at 800-805-5489 or specialsales@sterlingpublishing.com.

Distributed in Canada by Sterling Publishing
C/o Canadian Manda Group, 165 Dufferin Street
Toronto, Ontario, Canada M6K 3H6

Distributed in Australia by Capricorn Link (Australia) Pty. Ltd.
P.O. Box 704, Windsor, NSW 2756 Australia

Manufactured in China

Sterling ISBN 978-1-58816-775-0

Contents

Introduction

Hey, CosmoGirl! Your life is a great big adventure and you're the star: new friends to meet, bold challenges to tackle, and fantastic places to go. Finding out just who you are and what makes you tick may be the most important—and fun— adventure of all. After all, you're one of kind! But between school and activities, studies and work, family and friends, there's barely a moment to spare. Take a breather—it's good for you, we promise—and discover what kind of friend you are or what your secret power is—just two of the 120 quizzes collected here.

We know you love quizzes. And why not? They're a fun way to discover things you may not yet know about yourself. Questions about what kind of prom dress fits your personality, what color your aura is, and what kind of sandwich you are may seem silly, but they're just a different way of helping you look at yourself, your life, and your personality. Think about them a little bit and these questions can really help you figure out who you are and maybe even who you want to be.

This super-sized book collects all our best quizzes and gives you a great excuse to take some time to think about YOU in different ways. Grab a pencil and have fun with some of our quirky, interesting, fascinating quizzes—and remember, there are no wrong answers!

All About You

CosmoGIRL Fun

Inner Girl

fun fun fun fun fun fun fun fun
fun fun fun fun fun fun fun fun
fun fun fun fun fun fun fun fun
fun fun fun fun fun fun fun fun
fun fun fun fun fun fun fun fun
fun fun fun fun fun fun fun fun
fun fun fun fun fun fun fun fun
fun fun fun fun fun **fun** fun fun
fun fun fun fun fun fun fun fun
fun fun fun fun fun fun fun fun
fun fun fun fun fun fun fun fun
fun fun fun fun fun fun fun fun
fun fun fun fun fun fun fun fun
fun fun fun fun fun fun fun fun
fun fun fun fun fun fun fun fun
fun fun fun fun fun fun fun fun
fun fun fun fun fun fun fun fun
fun fun fun fun fun fun fun fun
fun fun fun fun fun fun fun fun
fun fun fun fun fun fun fun fun
fun fun fun fun fun fun fun fun
fun fun fun fun fun fun fun fun
fun fun fun fun fun fun fun fun
fun fun fun fun fun fun fun fun
fun fun fun fun fun fun fun fun
fun fun fun fun fun fun fun fun
fun fun fun fun fun fun fun fun

FIND YOUR POWER COLOR

Wear it. Write with it. Bathe in it (why not?) for that hit of energy that beats Starbucks any day!

1. Do you write in a journal?
a. Yes, every day.
b. I try, but I'm usually too busy to write it all down.
c. No, but I keep meaning to *start* one.
d. No. Bor-*ring.*

2. What's your favorite kind of movie?
a. An arty film (with subtitles, *s'il vous plaît!).*
b. A total tearjerker drama.
c. A revved-up action adventure flick.
d. A fun (stupid!) comedy.

3. Which airplane seat do you prefer?
a. It just depends on the mood I'm in.
b. A window seat.
c. The aisle, please!
d. Whatever they give me is just fine.

4. Which party game do you like best?
a. Ouija. Break out the board!
b. Truth or Dare.
c. Spin the Bottle. Need an Altoid, anyone?
d. Pictionary.

5. After school, you've got the energy to:
a. Hit the couch for a nap.
b. Just do my homework.
c. Make it through a meeting and practice.
d. Run a marathon, if only I had time.

6. What would you love to do on a Saturday?
a. Hang out in the park and catch up with a friend.
b. Volunteer for a really great cause.
c. Try an extreme sport.
d. Plan a last-minute party.

Add 'em up!

Give yourself 1 point for each a, 2 for each b, 3 for each c, and 4 for each d.

6–10 points: Blue You think about things deeply, and you don't mind if your strong opinions make waves. You always know what's right in your *heart*—that's why friends call you in a crisis. But to *keep* that stress away, get blue sheets or an ocean-toned screensaver to create a personal oasis.

11–15 points: Green You're down-to-earth and giving, not to mention supportive, which makes you a great friend. Even *guys* can reveal their problems to you—your ability to talk things through brings out everyone's peaceful side. To maintain *your* inner calm, write on green paper or with green ink.

16–19 points: Red Spontaneous and passionate, you go for the goal, whether it's the lead in a play *or* that cutie in History. But before you give something your all (a guy, a project, whatever), make sure your plan is realistic—it'll save you heartbreak later. And don't *hide* that fiery spirit. Fill up your closet with red accessories.

20–24 points: Yellow Hello, sunshine! You're one successful, smiley chica. Teachers love you, guys trust you, and you've got tons of friends. But remember, it *is* okay to be sad sometimes. Share your troubles with one of those many friends—you'll bounce back fast. Yellow can be hard to *wear,* but use a bright notebook for an energy infusion.

WHAT KIND OF CAR ARE YOU?

1. What's your dream destination?
a. The Colorado Rockies.
b. Hawaii.
c. Paris, but of course!
d. Vegas, baby.

2. Which dare would you take?
a. Running outside in the cold—in my undies!
b. Crank-calling: "Is Mr. Hugh Jass there?"
c. Asking out a stranger.
d. Mooning a passing car.

3. What's your favorite car color?
a. Forest green.
b. Deep blue.
c. Glittery gold.
d. Bright red.

4. Your best friend is having a party. She asks you to:
a. Make the food.
b. Invite people.
c. Decorate her place.
d. Make mix CDs.

5. Makeup is:
a. A pain.
b. Something I don't use much of.
c. A must.
d. Fun to play around with.

6. What's your perfect workout?
a. Hiking.
b. Running.
c. Yoga.
d. Kickboxing.

Add 'em up!

Give yourself 1 point for each a,
2 for each b, 3 for each c, and 4 for each d.

6–10 points: Range Rover

Whether you're off-roading or heading to the slopes, there's no challenge you can't handle. You're powerful and capable, and your positive energy is unbeatable. Just be sure to get enough "gas" (food and sleep) so you don't tire out too quickly.

11–15 points: BMW Sedan

You are one well-oiled machine—and you know you don't have to be the flashiest to be the best. You're all about reliability, loyalty, and making other people feel comfortable. Keep using your fabulous common sense and you'll be in great shape for the long run.

16–19 points: Mercedes-Benz Convertible

Every detail about your vehicle rocks. Sophisticated and versatile, you pack more than enough power to get you where you want to go (hint: It's far). Your challenge: Don't worry about little scratches and dings. Learn to sit back and enjoy the ride.

20–24 points: Porsche Carrera

You definitely live life in the fast lane. People get out of your way when you zoom by, and it's a good thing, because there's no stopping you once you get a great idea. But watch those speed limits—just because you can go fast doesn't mean you always should.

WHAT KIND OF SHOE ARE YOU?

Read on to meet your "sole" mate.

1. When someone asks what your favorite class is, you're quick to answer:
a. Sociology.
b. Study hall.
c. Gym.
d. Art.

2. If you had to get to school on just two wheels, you'd prefer to arrive on a:
a. Retro-new Schwinn.
b. Vespa.
c. Mountain bike.
d. Harley.

3. As a kid, your Barbie doll was usually:
a. Dressed impeccably.
b. Making out with Ken.
c. Enclosed in a dusty box under your bed.
d. Sporting a customized punk-rock hairdo.

4. When you get glammed up for a party, you want people to say you look like:
a. Reese Witherspoon.
b. Britney Spears.
c. Katie Holmes.
d. Avril Lavigne.

5. Which of these reality shows would you most want to be on?
a. *The Bachelorette*.
b. *The Real World*.
c. *Survivor*.
d. *Fear Factor*.

6. If you could have just one, which a.m. beverage would you drink?
a. Freshly squeezed o.j.
b. Cappuccino.
c. Fruit smoothie.
d. Red Bull.

Scoring*

mostly a's: Classic flat

You always seem poised, even if you have on safety gear in chem lab. That quality, like flats, is timeless—and it's why everyone knows they can always count on you. You know that true grace comes from being true to yourself.

mostly b's: Sexy stiletto

For you, there's no dress rehearsal, so you just sashay through life (looking great, we might add!). Risky and to-the-point (à la these heels), you're always ready for your close-up—hey, you want the attention you deserve!

mostly c's: Comfy sneaker

Your mission: to do it all. You bounce easily between activities—just like your favorite pair of trainers. There's always another adventure coming, so you'll always have new ways to stay occupied (and happy)!

mostly d's: Kick-butt boot

You're brave and will stomp all over convention . . . if you must. You leave your imprint everywhere, sorta like these thick-soled bad boys! Whether you're making a weird dish in home ec or shopping for clothes, you're always unique.

*End up with a tie? Just pick the description that best fits your personality.

WHAT ICE CREAM FLAVOR ARE YOU?

Listen—this is info you need to know!

1. On a Saturday afternoon, you'd most prefer:
a. Biking in the park.
b. Writing poetry and playing your guitar.
c. Scoping out cute guys at the mall.
d. Shopping with friends.

2. Which of these four female stars do you tend to identify with most?
a. Mandy Moore.
b. Alanis Morissette.
c. Alicia Keys.
d. Gwen Stefani.

3. You'd want to be famous for:
a. Saving an endangered species of animal.
b. Being the first female president—better look out, Barak Obama!
c. Designing dresses.
d. Throwing glam parties.

4. What's the one thing in your closet you love the most?
a. My comfy-slash-cute-slash-groovy sneakers.
b. My funky vintage jacket.
c. My sexy leather pants.
d. My funny conversation-starter T-shirt.

5. In school, what subject do you usually get the best grades in?
a. Biology.
b. History.
c. Art.
d. English.

6. Your dream guy kind of reminds you of:
a. Andy Roddick (that adorable tennis player).
b. Tobey Maguire.
c. Enrique Iglesias.
d. Ashton Kutcher.

Scoring

If you get a tie, consider yourself swirled!

mostly a's: Vanilla

Even though you're earthy, you're anything but plain. You're perfectly at ease in any situation—whether it's chatting up your boyfriend's mom or passing out Greenpeace flyers to strangers. And you look prettiest when your hair's in a ponytail and you're wearing no makeup.

mostly b's: Coffee

Your intensity gives everyone a buzz, Miss Coffee. You're smart, smart, smart, and you're a natural born leader (politics, anyone?). You like seeing things from lots of different points of view, and you know how to stand up for what you believe in. Is it any wonder you're totally addictive?

mostly c's: Chocolate X

Romantic, creative, and passionate, you're definitely chocolatey. You have the ability to make people melt by seeing deep within them—past the superficial stuff, right to the meaningful core. That means you're a girl with great friendships—and very intense loves.

mostly d's: Strawberry

Tangy and refreshing, you live life at a mile a minute. Your friends admire and adore you, and it's easy to see why: They love that you make them laugh and that you're always up for an unpredictable good time.

WHAT DECADE DO YOU BELONG IN?

*Vintage is about more than just clothes—
it's a way of life, baby!*

1. At a party, you're:

a. With your guitar, leading a group sing-along.
b. On the dance floor, shaking your thang.
c. Mingling! Making connections is key.
d. Playing DJ—everyone loves your taste in music.

2. What's so you?

a. A peasant top and cute flip-flops.
b. A one-shoulder top, bootleg pants, and a side order of gold jewelry.
c. A leather mini and an off-the-shoulder top.
d. A little black dress.

3. You'd be happy:

a. On a mountainside, communing with nature.
b. At a coffee shop, flirting with a cute new guy.
c. On a podium, accepting your class presidency.
d. In your room, IM-ing all of your friends.

4. Your absolute dream boyfriend:

a. Signs e-mails, "Peace!"
b. Has all the right clothes and can dance!
c. Is going to Harvard.
d. Cooks, speaks Italian, runs marathons, and has a sensitive side.

5. After college, you'd love to:

a. Join the Peace Corps.
b. Become an edgy fashion designer.
c. Work 100-hour weeks and make millions as an investment banker.
d. Own 100 Starbucks.

6. Which of these songs would you say is your personal motto?

a. "Good Day Sunshine"
b. "Dancing Queen"
c. "Girls Just Want to Have Fun"
d. "If It Makes You Happy"

Scoring

If you get a tie, read both categories that apply to you.

mostly a's: 1960s So maybe you don't actually own love beads, but now that we mention it, you're kind of tempted, right? You belong in the '60s! You're a romantic with a sensitive, soulful side. You care deeply about everything you do, whether it's saving the planet or just making a friend feel loved. You simply radiate positive energy—it's no wonder you belong in the decade of peace, love, and happiness.

mostly b's: 1970s Click your heels three times, and we'll take you home to Studio 54, you little disco diva. Well, we would if we could! You, dancing queen, are the life of any party—especially this little party called Life. Your '70s qualities are obvious off the dance floor too. People love your ability to make even the roughest days fun.

mostly c's: 1980s Just like Madonna (back when she wore bras as outerwear), you know what you want and how to get it. You ooze power, smarts, and strength—and that's why you're perfect for the big-spending, big-time '80s. (But don't worry, that doesn't mean you have to have big hair to match!) You love a challenge—whether it's going Ivy League or flirting with the cutest guy in the room. Go you!

mostly d's: 2000s With your innovative personality and intelligence, you belong right in the fast-track '00s. You may work hard, but you play hard too. Direct the school play? No problem. Organize a poetry reading? Piece of cake. You're a total multi-tasking diva, and you truly understand how to carpe diem.

WHAT'S YOUR INTERNAL WEATHER REPORT?

Get the barometer on your outlook, sister!

1. When a teacher asks for your parents' number, you just assume:

a. You're in trouble.
b. It's parent-teacher conference time.
c. She's making sure she has the right info.

2. Your bangs are growing out. When you pass a mirror, you go:

a. "Oh, sweet Lord! I need a headband."
b. "Mental note: I've gotta get this cut soon."
c. "I'm so moppet-chic!"

3. You want to see the Ice Capades; your friends say no way. You end up:

a. Watching it on TV.
b. Going with your mom. (She's no arts snob.)
c. Dragging your friends.

4. The girls at the musical tryouts all sing like Mariah. You secretly think:

a. I have no chance.
b. I'll make the chorus.
c. Hopefully I'll get the lead part!

5. You get a coupon for a free facial in the mail. You think:

a. Great. Somebody's telling me I have acne.
b. Hmm, would I have to buy something?
c. Free facial. Yay!

6. A guy at the arcade looks at you, so you:

a. Figure he likes your friend and feel ugly.
b. Ask your friend, "Did he just check me out?"
c. Smile and invite him to play air hockey.

Scoring

mostly a's: **Cloudy with possible thunderstorms**

You feel a breeze and assume a hurricane is coming! It's great that you have an emergency shelter in case of disaster—but learn to appreciate the sunny days. Write down what's great about you and ask your friends what they admire about you. Soon you'll see the brighter side of life: Yes, he could like you, you could win the class election, and you do have a chance of winning the lottery!

mostly b's: **Partly cloudy, partly sunny**

Hey, sometimes it will rain on your parade, so you try to remember to play in the raindrops. When sucky things happen—like a breakup, or bad grade—you address them, learn, and move on. You know that if you can stay positive, every day will have at least some good parts!

mostly c's: **Not a cloud in sight**

Chance of rain? What's that? Your ability to see the sun makes people wonder if you've ever gone through a tough time. It's great that you've got such a bright attitude—just pay attention to reality and pack a raincoat (a.k.a. backup plan) so you'll have it on the days when you really do need it. Until then . . . bask in the warmth!

DO YOU HAVE A SIXTH SENSE?

Find out if you've got special ESP powers just waiting to be developed.

1. Ever wake up just before your alarm?
a. I barely wake up after the alarm's been blaring for ten minutes!
b. Occasionally . . . but it usually just means I have to pee.
c. Definitely!

2. How often do you experience déjà vu?
a. Never.
b. It's happened once or twice.
c. I could swear you've asked me this before . . .

3. Do you believe in the power of tarot cards?
a. No more than my old UNO deck.
b. Not really, but they can be insightful.
c. Of course—wanna see my deck?

4. How do you usually make decisions?
a. I think them through, using pros and cons.
b. I base them on logic, unless my heart tells me not to.
c. I go with my gut.

5. Can you finish your friend's sentences?
a. Only when I'm listening to her tell the same story for the 200th time.
b. Now and then.
c. All the time!

6. Ever met someone you felt like you knew?
a. Oh, please—that doesn't happen.
b. Yeah, I think I know what you mean.
c. It was like that when I met my best friend!

Add 'em up!

Give yourself 1 point for each a, 2 for each b, and 3 for each c.

6–9 points: Princess of Pragmatism

The way you see it, if God meant for you to have a third eye, false lashes would come in packs of three! You're sensible and logical. But don't ignore your inner feelings—they may actually be trying to help. We're not saying to drop your rational sense altogether, but practice listening to your gut: Buy the first candy you're drawn to, even if you've never tried it before; skip a street that gives you the creeps. Soon, you'll see that a sixth sense is a totally practical tool.

10–14 points: Extra Perceptive

Your rational side may tell you that you're just a girl with good instincts. But give your intuition some credit—it's real. Next time you've got a dilemma (like a red vs. a black prom dress), try this: Say the sensible option out loud ("The black dress; it's cheaper."). Feel disappointed? You'll know in your heart you want the other— it'll make you happier in the long run. By trusting your instincts and your intellect you'll get the best of both worlds.

15–18 points: Totally Tuned In

Who needs a Magic 8-Ball with you around?! You're the type who takes a different road to the mall, only to hear later that there was a huge wreck on your usual route. And when it comes to guys, you can spot a player a mile away. But just because your gut tells you to do something doesn't mean it's always right (otherwise we'd all have hitchhiked to the Korn show). Try making pro and con lists to evaluate risks. But then, you knew we were going to say that, didn't you?

WHAT'S YOUR
METROPOLITAN MATCH?

Because every international woman of mystery needs a place to call home.

1. You'd rather get a gift card for a:
a. Psychic reading.
b. Spa day.
c. Beauty makeover.
d. Music store.

2. Which summer program is right for you?
a. A creative writing workshop.
b. An "essentials of pastry" class.
c. A Fortune-500 internship.
d. An outdoor-adventure course.

3. At a party, you'd break the ice with:
a. "Is this song a cover?"
b. "Any hot guys here?"
c. "Where'd you get that shirt?"
d. "Ready to start dancing?"

4. Which sounds like the best school field trip?
a. A hands-on pottery demo.
b. A cool museum.
c. A neighborhood walking tour.
d. One you take on senior-ditch day.

5. What snack would you make for your friends?
a. Veggie chili.
b. Chocolate-covered strawberries.
c. Pizza.
d. Nachos with mango salsa.

6. Your personality is most like that of a:
a. Chinchilla—you're unpredictable!
b. Cat—you love lounging in comfort.
c. Dog—you get excited easily.
d. Shark—who needs sleep?

Scoring

mostly a's: Prague

Feel that buzz? It's your indie spirit, alive in the city that gave birth to the boho lifestyle. Artists and philosophers flock here—kind of like they do to your living room on Friday nights. No wonder Prague's on your to-visit list.

mostly b's: Paris

Do we hear violins? A daydreamer like you belongs in the land of romantic ideals. High culture and fab art give you the sense that your chic fantasies have come true.

mostly c's: New York City

Who hearts NY? You! Crowds, shopping, celebs! Your flash-boom-bang personality is right at home. On the subway or in SoHo, one thing you won't be is bored.

mostly d's: Rio de Janeiro

Do you ever stop to *rest*? This is the ultimate fun town. Festivals, friendly guys, bare-to-there dress codes, and non-stop dancing make life the party you know it *can* be. Hey, why wear pants when bikini bottoms will do?

inner girl inner girl inner girl inner girl
girl inner girl inner girl inner girl
inner girl inner girl inner girl inner
girl inner girl inner girl inner girl
inner girl inner girl inner girl inner
girl inner girl inner girl inner girl
inner girl inner girl inner girl inner
girl inner girl inner girl inner girl
inner girl inner girl inner girl inner
girl inner girl inner girl inner girl
inner girl inner girl inner girl inner
girl inner girl inner girl inner girl
inner girl inner girl inner girl inner
girl inner girl inner girl inner girl
inner girl inner girl inner girl inner
girl inner girl inner girl inner girl
inner girl **inner girl** inner girl inner
girl inner girl inner girl inner girl
inner girl inner girl inner girl inner
girl inner girl inner girl inner girl
inner girl inner girl inner girl inner
girl inner girl inner girl inner girl
inner girl inner girl inner girl inner
girl inner girl inner girl inner girl
inner girl inner girl inner girl inner
girl inner girl inner girl inner girl
inner girl inner girl inner girl inner
girl inner girl inner girl inner girl

WHAT COLOR IS YOUR LOVE LIFE?

Discover the true hue of your crushing style—red-hot or not!

1. At a dance, you're probably the person:

a. Hanging with your girls.
b. Flirting with different peeps.
c. Dancing close with one guy.

2. Your first question for a love psychic would have to be:

a. "Will I ever get a guy?"
b. "Is he getting serious about me?"
c. "Will he be mine forever?"

3. You get a note from "a secret admirer" and:

a. Go, "psssh"—it's probably one of your friends being ridiculous.
b. Hope it's the guy you like.
c. Giggle and tell your guy thanks.

4. If you're single on Valentine's Day, you:

a. Aren't surprised.
b. Go out with your single friends (and maybe even meet a guy).
c. Get really depressed.

5. When prom time comes, you'll likely go with:

a. Your closest guy friend (he won't mind you gawking at your crush).
b. A cute guy you flirt with at work.
c. Your boyfriend—who else?

6. Major track meet coming up. You're excited to:

a. Check out the events.
b. Warm up with the triple-jumper you've had your eye on.
c. Give your crush a massage.

Scoring

mostly a's: Crushing coral

You browse through the grocery store of boys out there at times, but so far, your basket is empty. That's because guys aren't topping your list of priorities right now. Good for you that you're waiting to turn on your fiery side when the right guy catches your eye.

mostly b's: Passionate purple

You love love and getting swept off your feet! For you, life right now is about sampling many flavors. But you might be passing up a great guy without even knowing it. Ask friends for outside opinions on your love life if you need some perspective about Mr. Right versus Mr. Right Now. They'll help you know when to get serious.

mostly c's: Serious scarlet ✗

Caution: Contents are hot! Deep red is the hue of A Serious Thing, which is what you're always looking for (even if you don't have a special guy at this very instant). When you get involved, you open up your heart and world to that person. That's an amazing quality, and it leads to mature relationships. Red looks great on you!

WHY DON'T YOU HAVE A BOYFRIEND?

Find out why the only tush pocket your hand slips into is your own, cookie!

1. What do you do when you see that h-o-t soccer player who scored yesterday's winning goal?

a. Congratulate him on a good game.
b. Playfully pat his cute little butt, guys'-locker-room style.
c. Half smile and kind of look away.

2. Your older sister takes you to a party while you're visiting her at college. You:

a. Flirt with some cute guys.
b. Quietly people-watch on the porch.
c. Dance with her and her friends—you came to be with her, after all.

3. Your parents won't let your sister wear a strapless dress to her prom. You feel bad that she's upset and:

a. Lobby hard-core on her behalf. Why shouldn't she wear what she wants?
b. Say nothing—why rock the boat?
c. Take her shopping—why not find one she and your parents will like?

4. The envelope arrives, and—drum roll, please!—you totally rocked your SATs! You:

a. Bring up your score every chance you get at school the next day.
b. Excitedly tell the people you feel closest to.
c. Tell just your parents—you don't want to rub it in your friends' faces.

5. Which best describes what you do when the yearbook comes out at the end of each school year?

a. Flip through it when you first get it and then lose it in your locker.
b. Carry it in your backpack in case someone asks to sign it.
c. Ask everyone you know to sign it using your funky-colored pens.

6. You're selling M&Ms for a charity fund-raiser. When you find out your principal is a candy freak, you:

a. Walk by her office—but then decide not to bother her after all.
b. Schedule a quick visit with her through her secretary.
c. Pop into her office during lunch and give her your best sales pitch.

7. You have plans to hang out with the girls on Friday night, but your crush calls to ask you to a movie. You:

a. Say yes—if you say no this time, he might never call again, right?
b. Say yes—your friends know your drop-everything-for-guys rule!
c. Say you can't do it Friday, but how about Saturday instead?

Answer Key

1: a = 2, b = 3, c = 1;	5: a = 2, b = 1, c = 3;
2: a = 3, b = 1, c = 2;	6: a = 1, b = 2, c = 3;
3: a = 3, b = 1; c = 2;	7: a = 1, b = 3, c = 2
4: a = 3, b = 2, c = 1;	

Scoring

Figure out your score to reveal why "us"-ness hasn't come your way—yet.

7-11 points: You're bashful!

You're pretty self-sufficient and are more into doing things one-on-one than in a big group. But lying low means that people (read: guys) may not get to see just how fabulous you are. So start taking small risks every now and then. Next time a cute guy catches your eye, flash that great smile of yours at him and say hi!

12-16 points: You're booked!

You feel secure in yourself, and your friends and interests fill up most of your time. You don't need a guy to make you feel special. But the kind of person who will make you happiest when you're ready will probably be someone who appreciates all of your passions and who has similar interests too.

17-21 points: You're bold!

Amazing opportunities have come to you because you rarely back away from what you want! But not all guys are right for your strong personality. Believe it or not, a shy guy might be your best bet—he'll appreciate your take-charge attitude and the fact that you can say exactly what you mean.

DO YOU ACT YOUR AGE?

Find out if you belong in a nursery—or a nursing home!

1. A friend lends you her John Mayer CD on Thursday and asks you to return it on Sunday. You:

a. Can't find it. But you'll buy her a new one before Sunday.
b. Think it's somewhere in your car; you'll try to make time to find it.
c. Totally flake—you lent it to another friend without thinking.
d. Have it waiting for her at her house, just like you promised.

2. Mom and Dad have to work late and ask you to get yourself and your kid brother dinner. You:

a. Chow down on a Twinkie feast and plop in front of the TV.
b. Go through the fridge and whip up turkey burgers and salads.
c. Head to Mickey D's for two quarter pounders—with cheese!
d. Take your brother out to get sandwiches and ice cream.

3. What did you do with last year's $100 birthday check from Gram and Gramps?

a. Lost it in your room and asked them if they'd mind writing a new one.
b. Cashed it ASAP and headed to the mall for a shopping spree.
c. Put half in the bank and spent the other $50 on makeup and hair stuff.
d. Deposited it in your savings account so that it could start earning interest.

4. Your doctor takes the cast off your broken ankle and tells you to wear comfy shoes for a while. You:

a. Wear nothing but your cushy sneakers for the next month.
b. Wear ballet flats; okay, they're not orthopedic, but they're flat, right?
c. Wear your boots with the small motorcycle heel.
d. Wear your cool high-heel platforms; any other shoe would kill your style.

5. When your boss catches you showing up 15 minutes late for work, you:

a. Apologize and make up a white lie about hitting unexpected traffic.
b. Mumble, "Sorry," then complain to coworkers that she's a tyrant.
c. Make up some kooky story about helping a friend with an emergency.
d. Look her in the eye, apologize, and tell her it won't happen again.

6. Your parents are trusting you to stay home alone this weekend while they're at a wedding. You:

a. Send out an Evite for everyone to stop by Saturday night.
b. Invite a small group of friends over to hang out.
c. Use the extra quiet time to work on all those college essays.
d. Wear pajamas all weekend and watch movies on Lifetime.

Answer Key

1: a = 3, b = 2, c = 1, d = 4;

2: a = 1, b = 4, c = 2, d = 3;

3: a = 1, b = 2; c = 3, d = 4;

4: a = 4, b = 3, c = 2, d = 1;

5: a = 3, b = 1, c = 2, d = 4;

6: a = 1, b = 2, c = 4, d = 3

Scoring

Do some quick math to see whether you act your age . . . or your shoe size.

6-9 points: Babe In Toyland

You still have that totally carefree attitude you had in grade school. Sometimes you don't consider the effects of your actions; start weighing pros and cons before just jumping into big decisions.

10-14 points: Kid At Heart

You're free-spirited—and refreshing to be around! But adults may be wary of giving you too much freedom because you seem distracted. Prove your reliability by following through more often.

15-19 points: Teen (In) Spirit

You have fun without being reckless and can see others' perspectives, which is why people are drawn to you. Just make sure you continue to balance responsibility with having a good time.

20-24 points: Woman At Work

You're responsible and always do the "right" thing. But make sure that you can recognize good risks from bad ones. That way you won't be held back in life for fear of "messing up."

WHAT KIND OF DAUGHTER ARE YOU?

Do your neighbors wish you were theirs?
Or do they count their blessings that you're not?

1. Your curfew is:

a. Not an issue—I'm home by then anyway.
b. Not negotiable.
c. More of an ETA, since I'm sometimes late.
d. A joke.

2. What's the main reason to get A's?

a. So I don't get in trouble.
b. So I can get into college.
c. Because I feel good about myself when I do well.
d. There is no reason.

3. The summer job you'd want is:

a. Babysitting.
b. Working at the mall.
c. Volunteering at an animal shelter.
d. Roadie for a rock group.

4. Do you ever clean around the house?

a. Of course, we all help.
b. Yes, I have chores.
c. When it gets messy.
d. Yeah—I clean out the cabinets by snacking!

5. Which character do you identify with?

a. Sweet Lucy on *7th Heaven.*
b. Thoughtful *Felicity.*
c. Fun Phoebe on *Charmed.*
d. Rebel Jen on *Dawson's Creek.*

6. Could you go far away for college?

a. No way! Too scary.
b. Yes, if that's where the best school is.
c. Sure, I'd like to.
d. Could I? I can't wait to!

Scoring

Give yourself 1 point for every a, 2 for every b, and 3 for every c. Now add `em up.

6-10 points: Mama & Daddy's Little Girl

Your parents are as much a part of your decisions as your friends. You can talk to them about almost anything. But don't worry about pushing the rules a little—that's part of growing up, and your parents will love your independent side too.

11-15 points: First Daughter X

You're responsible, trustworthy, and you make Mom and Dad proud. As long as you're trying hard because you want to (not just to please the folks), you'll be successful at all you do. Even when you do something wild, your parents still know you respect them (because you actually ask before you dye your hair blue!).

16-19 points: Independent Offspring

You have a good relationship with your parents—you know they'll always be behind you. Since they trust you, they're happy to let you go for your goals, even if it means you might move far away.

20-24 points: Wild Child

You want to live your life your way—and who can blame you? But next time you feel penned in by parental rules, think about why they exist (to keep you safe!). Show them that you have good judgment—they'll trust you and be more likely to extend that curfew!

Your mom thinks you're beautiful. Your friends say you're the best. But what is that guy thinking?

1. You're at a Friday-night party relaxing on the couch with friends when (yes—just as you'd hoped) your crush walks in. What do you do?

a. Find a way to ditch your friends (they'll understand, right?), and go over and talk to him before some other girl corners him.

b. Catch his eye, smile and wave, and then go right back to talking to your friends (for now, anyway).

c. Avoid eye contact while sending him mental "I like you" vibes.

2. Same party. So, who is it you're hanging out with on that couch mentioned in the first question?

a. Either all of your girlfriends or a bunch of guy friends.

b. Some girls, some guys.

c. Your best friend, you're having an intense one-on-one discussion.

3. Okay, we promise this will be the last party question: What, most likely, are you wearing?

a. Short skirt, tight top—it's a party!

b. Your sexiest jeans, a cute party top, and maybe a little extra lip stuff.

c. Probably the same thing you wore to school that day.

4. If you had to sum up your entire life's relationship history with guys, you'd say you've had:

a. A few summer flings, at least three boyfriends since the beginning of high school, and your fair share of hookups on weekends.

b. Lots of guy friends, zero to three boyfriends, and maybe one or two (max!) hookups (or none at all).

c. One really serious long-term boyfriend or crush, and not very many guy friends.

5. So there you are, sitting in calc class directly behind your crush, when you notice that (ay, ay, ay!) his tag is sticking out of the back of his shirt. What do you do?

a. Relish the opportunity to fix it and let your fingers oh so casually linger on his gorgeous neck for a couple of seconds longer.

b. Whisper, "Hey, your tag's sticking out," and then quickly tuck it in with a cute little pat.

c. Just do nothing—even if you do (go ahead, admit it!) daydream about massaging his neck.

6. How would you describe your friends (i.e., the people he sees you with every day)?

a. A big but tight circle. You eat lunch, study, and party together.

b. A few different groups: your best friends, your team-mates, and of course, your HBO-addict friends.

c. An extremely close small group.

7. Be honest: When it comes to guys, do you think it's accurate to say that you have a "type"?

a. Yes! All the guys you've liked tend to fit into the same physical mold.

b. Sure, but in more of a personality way than a physical one.

c. Not really. Every guy you've liked is totally different from the last.

Scoring

Give yourself 3 points for every a, 2 for every b, and 1 for every c. Now add 'em up.

17–21 points: Intimidating

You're outgoing, fun, and popular. But . . . the guys who are gutsy enough to approach you can be cockier than a rooster on Viagra (scary!). And nicer guys are afraid you'll reject them. To make them relax, try a new activity so they'll see that you like being with people other than your usual crowd. Also, turn down your flirting a notch. Just waving to him at a party can give him the confidence to come up to *you*.

12–16 points: Sweet

You've got self-confidence, and guys flock to that like mice to cheese fondue. By hanging out with people in different crowds, looking your best but not overdoing it, and being a mix of friendly and flirty, you show guys you're interested in them as people. P.S. If you're into a guy friend, be a little flirtier so he knows you're *not* just one of the guys.

7–11 points: Mysterious

You're private, so guys who like you can't tell enough *about* you to know what to say. If you like him, help him! Mention something you have in common: "I hear you like fly-fishing. My dad and I just went." Don't know him well? Bring up a current event. Hey, even a *smile* can show him you'd like to talk.

Do you roll with the punches or spark up drama?

1. Your family vacation to the Bahamas is canceled because of the hurricane. You . . .

a. Roll your eyes and mutter "This really sucks" loud enough for your parents to hear, then slam your bedroom door.

b. Freak out. Your entire spring break is ruined because you'll be the only one to go back to school without a tan.

c. Shrug it off. At least you found out about the storm before you spent your entire allowance on a new bikini. Phew!

2. You drop a huge tray of glasses while waiting on tables. You . . .

a. Tell your boss it was the stupid busboy's fault for leaving the floor wet.

b. Turn bright red and start to cry.

c. Bow and thank the customers for their applause, then promise your manager you'll be more careful in the future.

3. Your father's company is relocating your family from sunny California to a tiny ski town thousands of miles away. You . . .

a. Tell your parents they're crazy if they think you're moving to Nowheresville. Military school sounds like more fun.

b. Kiss your social life goodbye. These are supposed to be the best years of your life, but now they'll be the worst!

c. Can't wait to check out the cute guys on the slopes.

4. Your friend is throwing a huge April Fools' Day costume party and you need a getup. You . . .

a. Boycott the bash. Dressing up in silly costumes is so not your idea of a good time.

b. Spend hours on the night of the party frantically hunting around in your mom's closet for something—anything—to wear.

c. Get in the spirit by dressing up as a zombie cheerleader.

5. Your best bud starts dating a cute guy from another school. When she tells you about their super-romantic date, you think:

a. "Could she be sappier? All this lovey-dovey stuff is making me nauseous."

b. "She's so perfect—all she has to do is look at a guy and he's fully in love with her. I'll never have a boyfriend."

c. "How amazing for her! I can't wait until someone takes me on a date like that!"

6. The first college you get a response from turns you down. Your immediate reaction is:

a. "How could they reject me? That loser from down the block got in last year . . . "

b. "I'm a total failure. I'll probably end up living with my parents forever."

c. "Oh shoot! It's a good thing I applied to a bunch of different schools."

7. Your math teacher springs a pop quiz on you and you know you bombed it. You . . .

a. Complain to your mom that your teacher is way too harsh—and has it in for you.

b. Throw a fit after class and tell your teacher she must let you take it again. This time you promise you'll do well!

c. Plan on doing extra credit. There's got to be a way you can save your grade.

Scoring

Give yourself 1 point for every a, 2 points for every b, and 3 points for every c.

17 to 21 points: Super-positive Girl

Even when you're majorly embarrassed or really disappointed, you focus on finding a solution, not wallowing in the problem. But sometimes you stifle your feelings just to keep everyone else happy. If something bad happens, spill your guts to a trusted pal. Expressing your emotions will make you feel better—plus, you'll get to bond with your bud.

12 to 16 points: The Drama Queen

You make a big deal out of *everything*. But constantly freaking out is exhausting. To help figure out what is—and what's not—worth your energy, start keeping a journal. Every time catastrophe strikes, write it down and at the end of a month, reread your entries. You'll realize that only one (okay, maybe two) of your freak-outs was truly legit. The rest were minor glitches that now seem silly. Soon you'll be solving probs with solutions instead of stressful sob sessions.

7 to 11 points: Miss Cranky-Pants

You're never afraid to say what you think—but you usually think everything sucks. When you're always looking for the downside, you don't open yourself up to anything good that might happen. To tune up your 'tude, try this: Every time you say something nasty, put a dollar in a jar. As the money piles up, you'll realize how often you're not so nice. Then use the cash to do something sweet for the people you've been mean to.

WHAT DO PEOPLE THINK OF YOU?

You're not paranoid for wanting to know.
You're human.

This quiz is designed to show you how other people see you and what you can do if that's not who you really are inside. Answer these Qs according to what you'd actually do, not what you wish you'd do. Then read on to find out if the impression you give truly reflects the inner you. If not, we'll show you how to bring out the side you're hiding, so the world can see your real amazing self!

1. You're cruising in your car with your friends and you accidentally hit the car in front of you. You:

a. Sit there in shock.
b. Flip out and yell at the other driver.
c. Roll your eyes and pull over.
d. Get out and start exchanging your insurance info with the other driver.

2. You're sitting in class, and the teacher asks a question you totally know the answer to. What do you do?

a. Let someone else answer it, in case you're wrong.
b. Just blurt the answer right out.
c. Don't answer—you're too busy drawing in your notebook to bother.
d. Raise your hand.

3. It's 3 p.m. You and your friends are in the school hallway. Your crush is approaching, so you:

a. Quickly turn and talk to your friends so he won't realize you noticed him.
b. Keep talking to your friends, and then bust on his outfit (in a funny way) when he walks by.
c. Stare him down as he passes you to see if you can catch his eye.
d. Wait until he gets near you, smile, and say, "Hi, Jake, what's up?"

4. A friend calls to tell you about a new guy she likes and goes on and on (and on!) about it. So you:

a. Let her talk for as long as she wants.

b. Say, "That sounds just like me and _____ (your crush's name)!"

c. Listen for a few minutes before you get bored and start flipping through the TV channels while she talks.

d. Cut to the chase by saying, "So are you going to call him?"

5. You're clothes shopping, and you need a different size. The salesperson keeps ignoring you to help other customers. You:

a. Just stand there patiently, hoping she'll look at you sometime soon.

b. Clear your throat loudly and start complaining to your friend.

c. Get annoyed and leave—that shirt was too preppy looking, anyway.

d. Walk over and say, "Excuse me, is there someone who can help me?"

6. There's a college fair at your school over the weekend, and everyone is "strongly encouraged" to go. You:

a. Go and walk around quietly collecting brochures. If you have questions, you'll just call later.

b. Grab some stuff in the first five minutes, then start talking to some of the other kids about which colleges have the best party scenes.

c. Don't go—the alternative kinds of schools you'll be applying to probably won't be there anyway.

d. Go, armed with a list of questions to ask the admissions people at all five of your top-choice schools.

7. Your friend begs you to go to the Fake Brain concert with her, but you're so not into them. You:

a. Go anyway to be a good friend.

b. Tell her you'll go as long as she'll agree to hang out after the show and get some pizza with your friends.

c. Tell her sorry, you'd rather get a Brazilian bikini wax. (Youch!)

d. Tell her no thanks, but name three people you know would love to go.

Scoring

The letter you chose the most reflects the way people see you. Got a tie between two or even three letters? Ask a friend if she thinks you chose the right answers for you. But it's possible you could be a mix of types— so read each with an open mind and see which one sounds the most like you.

mostly a's: Miss Introspective

First impression? Quiet and observant, you let others take the lead. You're seen as a shy girl, but also as a caring, considerate friend—the one everyone comes to when they need a shoulder to cry on. You're happy to listen to your friends, and you're never pushy with your opinions— you keep them to yourself. People tend to wonder what thoughts lie behind your knowing eyes.

Doesn't sound like the REAL you? Just because you're quiet doesn't mean you haven't got some totally wild ideas brewing in your head! So get ready to surprise people with them.

Tip 1: Practice speaking your mind. After you're in a group situation, write down what you were feeling and what (or who) may have stopped you from saying or doing what you wanted. Also write down the things you wanted to say or do but didn't. Knowing exactly what those thngs are is almost like planning for what you'll do in the future. Next time, wait for those short pauses in the conversation, then jump in with your thoughts or opinions.

Tip 2: When you're in a big group, make sure you stand toward the center of the crowd. People will expect to hear more from you, so you'll be forced to let your thoughts loose more often.

Tip 3: Try to take more chances. Go to a café alone or join a club at school that none of your good friends are in. Once you're out of the shadows of your crowd, you'll have to speak up. Soon you'll be more comfortable letting your inner self shine.

mostly b's: Social Butterfly

First impression? Outgoing and extroverted, you've got lots of friends in all different groups. People have stereotyped you as a party girl because you're always up for doing something social, and you're the one who always knows the plan for Saturday night. Since you're not afraid to open your mouth to express an opinion or tell someone what you think of them, people feel there's never a dull moment when you're around. Doesn't sound like the REAL you? You know how you always read interviews with celebrities known for lavish partying and they say, "That's so not me—I'm really down-to-earth"? You may be kind of like that—you feel totally laid-back and yet for some reason everyone thinks you're this wild party girl. Here's how to let people see more of your serious side.

Tip 1: As great as you are at it, resist the urge to entertain! Next time you want to give your shocking or sassy opinion, pause and count to three. Is it really worth it? If so, go for it! But look at every opportunity as a chance to give a more thoughtful or heartfelt (instead of just crazy!) opinion instead.

Tip 2: Stand on the edge of the group instead of in the middle, at least some of the time. That makes others take the floor, and you'll get to take a nice break from always being the center of attention.

Tip 3: Once a weekend, hang out with your closest friends doing something low-key. Don't feel you're letting people down by not showing up at a party. Sometimes being offstage can remind you what it feels like to be the real you.

mostly c's: Independent Woman

First impression? Some people who don't know you might think you're a little standoffish, since you don't usually make the first move to talk to them. You're known around school as the girl who doesn't seem to care what anyone else thinks and doesn't feel the need to belong. Since you go your own way in what you wear, the music you listen to, and most other things, too, people think you're totally over all the stuff they're still insecure about.

Doesn't sound like the REAL you? Sometimes the people who seem totally "cool" and alternative on the outside are as cuddly as teddy bears on the inside. You can make yourself just a little more approachable too, if that's what you want.

Tip 1: Use your passions to connect with people. If you're an environmentalist, organize a peaceful protest against deforestation; if you design jewelry, start selling it. This way, you'll interact with people, and they'll see the real girl behind your cool facade.

Tip 2: You might think school clubs are so not you, but if you get involved in one that you can get into, you might be surprised to find out that even kids who look the most "mainstream" on the outside are nice and weird (in a good way—the way we all are!) once you know them.

Tip 3: Try not to separate yourself from the crowd just to prove you won't conform. If you get the urge to go to a school dance and boogie to BSB songs, don't not do it because it doesn't go along with your image. Seeing you at a dance is the last thing anyone would expect of you, so you're still being your rebellious self. Ha!

mostly d's: Organizational Queen

First impression? You are goal-oriented and driven—the girl who people see as totally mature beyond high school. You're the one your friends come to when they've got a problem that needs solving—fast. They respect you for being so put together, but sometimes they wish you'd make more time to just kick back and relax.

Doesn't sound like the REAL you? Maybe you've got this fun-loving person inside who you haven't let out much since school keeps you way too busy. If you'd rather fit more of your fun self into your college-bound schedule, here's what you can do.

Tip 1: Take lessons with a friend in something noncompetitive—like pottery or baking. Don't worry about being the best at it—in fact, choose a hobby that you may kind of suck at. (C'mon, you can find something!) The point is to just have fun.

Tip 2: Since you're a great organizer, plan one activity a month for you and your friends where there's no purpose other than to make fools of yourselves and laugh your butts off (karaoke or bowling would be perfect!).

Tip 3: Show your friends that you can direct your energy toward being a friend just as well as you can put it toward acing an exam. If you really are busy when a friend calls, tell her you'll call her at a certain time later, and when it's that time, put aside what you're doing and give her your full attention. It'll give you a break and help her out too.

FIND YOUR INNER PARTY ANIMAL

Figure out your social prowess and work it!

1. If you planned an end-of-school event, it would be:

a. A "school's out" film fest: *Summer School, Dazed and Confused, Heathers,* etc.
b. Trading yearbooks at a fun restaurant.
c. A tiki-theme beach party.

2. If you're not dancing at a school function, it's because . . .

a. I'm waiting for someone to physically force me to.
b. I'm just waiting till the party really gets going.
c. I'm too busy talking with my friends.

3. Have you ever made out at a party?

a. No way—I think that's really tacky.
b. Yeah, but only playing party games and stuff.
c. Um, yeah. Hasn't everyone?

4. At a good club, there are always lots of:

a. Cushy couches to hang out on.
b. Square feet, so me and my friends can claim our own space.
c. People, even after it gets late.

5. At a friend's b-day bash, you spend the most time:

a. Getting to know one of her other friends better.
b. Catching up with my five best friends.
c. Running around, trying to find time to say hi to everyone.

6. It's a Friday night fiesta. What are you wearing?

a. Whatever I had on at school that day.
b. A comfortable (but really pretty!) outfit.
c. My amazing tube top and skirt—where else can I wear them?!

Add 'em up!

Give yourself 1 point for each a, 2 for each b, and 3 for each c.

6–9 points: Lone Wolf

At big events, you show up, say hi, and split when your ears start ringing. But that doesn't mean you're not social—hello! You'd just rather pair off for one-on-one hangouts. If you do find yourself stuck at a huge party, just get comfortable by chatting with a few select people.

10–14 points: Laid-Back Lion

You travel in a pack at parties, so you always have fun (whether the soirée is cool or not). You also know your own moods—if you don't want to go out, you won't show up and be miserable, you'll just rent videos with friends. Take a turn organizing big stuff too—reserve a table at a pizza place for a low-effort chance at party-planning.

15–18 points: Social Butterfly

Every time you talk to someone at a party, they think to themselves, "I should hang out with her more!" You're an expert match-maker, and you always make everyone in a group feel welcome. Make it a goal to spend time individually with the people you meet too.

If you were a bagel, would you be plain or everything? Hmm . . .

1. Midnight. Sleepover party. Truth or Dare. You pick:

a. Dare.
b. Truth.
c. Neither, you totally hate that game.

2. A motivational speaker who's trying to teach your school an "important lesson" whips out a bungee cord, asks for volunteers, and looks right at you. You:

a. Jump out of your seat and head right to the front of the auditorium.
b. Laugh nervously. If she picks you, you'll have to suck it up and go up.
c. Hide behind the big-headed kid sitting in the row in front of you.

3. At a party, you talk to a cutie all night. You two don't make out, but you do seem to have chemistry.

(Go, you!) Afterward, when your friends grill you for details, you:

a. Tell them every little detail of his life, including his latest chem grade and what he had for lunch that day.
b. Give them just the juiciest highlights of your conversation.
c. Shrug and say, "I dunno, he's cool."

4. How often do you change the way your bedroom looks (by putting up new posters, moving furniture around, etc.)?

a. At least a couple of times a year. You're always up for a new look.
b. Maybe once a year or so, when you're feeling particularly inspired.
c. Every few years. The last time was back when the Macarena was cool.

5. Think fast. How many after-school activities are you signed up for?

a. More than 3.
b. 1–3.
c. 0.

6. Let's just say you're having dinner at a friend's house, and her parents serve something you've never had (or even seen) before. What do you do?

a. Try it! (You never know— maybe you'll even ask for seconds.)
b. Try it (but only to be polite).
c. Take some, but shove it around your plate and hope nobody notices.

7. Crunch time! You've got one week to get ready for a big oral report on mountain climbing (a topic you know practically nothing about). You:

a. Take a climbing class and write about your first-person experience.
b. Do research and check out the local gear shop to talk to some expert climbers about their adventures.
c. Read some stuff on the Internet and write up the how-to.

Scoring

mostly a's: Wild Woman

You couldn't be boring if you tried. Sailing? Why not? Cool new club? Sure! Driving a convertible in the snow? Um, yeah. Well . . . sometimes your sense of adventure can get the best of you. So, if you're about to try something wild, stop and ask yourself if you really want to do it for you—not just to impress other people.

Dare: The next time a friend of yours is sad, use your wild instincts to cheer her up. Pick out crazy vintage clothes together at a thrift store and wear them out dancing that night!

mostly b's: Fun Compadre

You're adventurous enough to try to get backstage after an awesome concert or perfectly happy just listening to CDs with a friend. You're confidently spontaneous, willing to be wild one day and tame the next, and that makes people like you. They know the real you, and you get the amazing feeling of knowing they like you just as you are.

Dare: List the three most "boring" things in your life (like Saturday SAT class or babysitting for the Blues Clues–addicted Johnson twins, again), then figure out a way to make them exciting—like asking Mrs. Johnson if you can take her darling girls to the movies!

mostly c's: Miss Consistent

You're kind, loyal, and rock steady, and people love you for it. But if you change your routine, you'll have more fun. Sure, always ordering chicken parm is fine now, but eventually you will get sick of it. And (not to freak you out) if you always hang out with the same crowd, what if you get sick of them? So shake things up! Be bold! Order eggplant parmigiana and go to a par-tay this weekend.

Dare: Any time you're about to do something automatically, change it just a wee bit. You never know when a "happy accident" (like meeting a new guy at the Coke machine—not the Pepsi machine) could rock your world!

WHAT TYPE OF FRIEND ARE YOU?

Reveal the reasons why your best pals think you're so great!

___ It seems like your best friend and her boyfriend are always fighting. Their latest spat was five minutes ago. Give yourself one point if you're already on your way to her house with a box of Kleenex and pint of B&J; two points if you're on the phone with her telling her to lose the loser already; three points if you tell her you're on the other line, but you'll call her back in two minutes.

___ It's Friday night and you're cruising around with your usual crowd. Add one point if you're going to be the group's chauffeur (again!); two points if you agree to drive—if everyone chips in for gas; three points if you secretly love to drive because that means you can hit every party you want!

___ Your friend is on the verge of failing French. Add one point if you put aside your own studying to be her personal tutor; two points if you suggest she drop a few of her many extracurricular activities and make time to hit the books; three points if you round up a bunch of friends to take her to Rock 'n' Bowl and get her mind off it.

___ You and your best friend were invited to what's already being called the Party of the Year. The problem? Her heinous ex is going too. Give yourself one point if you pass on the party and go to a movie with your friend instead; two points if you try to get the party's host to disinvite the ex; three points if you convince your B.F. to put on a happy face—and a hot outfit—and party hearty.

_____ It's your birthday and your Gram stuffed your card with cash. Now you can: lend [insert broke friend's name here] that money she needs (add one point); buy yourself that MAC lipstick you've been eyeing (add two points); go with all your friends to see 'N Sync in concert (add three points).

_____ You hear the phone ring, and your mom says, "It's for you..." Chances are: someone in one of your classes wants to borrow your notes (add one point); a girlfriend needs your immediate attention to help decode her crush's recent strange behavior (add two points); a conference call awaits—two of your best buds want to know what's up for the weekend (add three points).

_____ You'd planned a mellow night at home when your friend calls and asks you to take over her babysitting gig so she can go out with her crush. Add one point if you happily volunteer—hey, at least you'll make a little extra cash; two points if you agree to fill in—after suggesting she return the favor by lending you her new black dress for the next big party; three points if you say "Okay—but only if I can invite some people to come over and hang."

_____ A friend asks to borrow $10, clearly forgetting she owes you $20 from last month. Add one point if you fork over the dough and figure you'll remind her later; two points if you say "Hello, I don't have 10 bucks—I lent you 20 last month, and you still haven't paid me back"; three points if you give it to her, but only after finding out that she needs it so she can go to the movies with you.

_____ You get a mass e-mail inviting you to a friend's party on Saturday night—tons of cool people will be there. The first thing you think is: "Wonder if they'll need any help setting up" (add one point); "Wonder if they know I really don't like huge parties" (add two points); "Wonder if they'll let me bring my crew too" (add three points).

Scoring

22 to 27 points: The Social Director

Fun is your middle name. You're the plan maker of the pack—and you wouldn't have it any other way! But if you don't remember to carve some solo space on your social calendar, you might get burned out. Don't ever stop having good times; just be sure to hang out alone every once in a while so you can relax and refuel.

15 to 21 points: The Straight Shooter

You're the ultimate go-to girl for thoughtful advice and truly honest opinions. Keep in mind, though, that while honesty is almost always the best policy, there's a fine line between just right and too harsh. The next time you're tempted to meddle in someone's business (or offer an opinion that wasn't asked for), stop and think about how you would feel if the tables were turned. If the answer is "not great," keep your advice to yourself.

9 to 14 points: The Giver

You're always just a phone call away when a friend needs help. Naturally, your gentleness and generosity make you majorly in demand as a best friend. Just don't become a doormat for friends with problems—sometimes you need to ask for help solving your probs too.

ARE YOU ANNOYING?

Find out what people really think of you.

1. The last time a friend confided in you about a problem and asked for your advice, you:

a. Told her what you thought she wanted to hear.
b. Got all the details, gave it some thought, then tried to offer a few helpful suggestions.
c. Listened, then told her about how the same thing had happened to you.

2. On the first day of class your teacher asks you to play the "get to know your neighbor" game. You:

a. Let her go first—you don't want her to think you're self-centered.
b. Ask her a few questions first, then share some stuff about yourself.
c. Tell her *everything*—who you're dating, where you were born, what your favorite color is—and before you know it, the bell rings.

3. Which one of the following TV teens would most people compare you with?

a. Willow (on *Buffy the Vampire Slayer*)—she gets along with everybody.
b. Elena (on *Felicity*)—she's got her own stuff to deal with, but she's still there when a friend needs help.
c. Nicole (on *Popular*)—she's not shy about letting everyone know exactly what she wants.

4. You're hanging out at your friends' house after school listening to some BSB. When you get hungry, you:

a. Wait until you get home to eat. You don't want to bother her parents by asking for a snack.
b. Tell your friend you're hungry and then eat whatever she offers.
c. Head straight for the kitchen and raid her fridge.

5. You like your friend's ex, and you feel like this is more than a crush—this could be the real thing. You:

a. Do nothing. A friend's ex is *totally* off-limits no matter what.
b. Talk to your friends about it before making a move.
c. Go for it! Hey, all's fair in love and war.

6. Your best friend gets a radical new haircut. When she asks you to give her your honest opinion of her new look, you:

a. Tell her you love it—after all, she can't change it *now*.
b. Try to figure out what she's feeling first—if she loves it, great; if not, reassure her that it'll grow out fast.
c. Love it so much you race to that salon to get yours done exactly the same!

7. When you and your friends head out in a group, how do you decide where you'll go and what you'll do?

a. You're fine with doing whatever everybody else wants.
b. It's tough making a plan, but you always seem to manage to get everyone to agree on something.
c. You usually try to convince your gang to go to any place where you think you might run into your crush.

Scoring

mostly a's: Eager to please

You're not annoying *enough*! It's nice that you're so tuned in to others' needs and feelings, and that you're so careful not to say anything that could be hurtful to anyone. But there are times when you really should be a bit more assertive with your *own* thoughts and desires. Sure, you want everyone to *like* you (who doesn't?), but you don't want to let people walk all over you. Come on, asking a friend for a drink when you're thirsty isn't exactly making a pest of yourself!

mostly b's: Gets the hint

You're not too pushy, but you're no *pushover* either. You pay attention to the signals your friends are giving out without letting them automatically have their way all the time. Friends probably think of you as a peacemaker because you're so good at listening to both sides and finding some way to get everybody to agree. And you also know that sometimes a little white lie is the best way to keep the peace—just be careful not to get carried away with those flattering fibs!

mostly c's: All about me!

The good news is, you're not afraid to stand up for yourself and ask for what you really want (*and* you usually get it). Of course you don't mean for your assertiveness to be annoying, but sometimes it can make you seem a little too self-absorbed. Even your closest friends might get kind of tired of feeling like they always have to do what *you* want to do. Try tuning in better to the signals your friends are giving out—you may find that going along with *their* plans sometimes is actually a lot of fun!

ARE YOU A SUCKER?

Take this quiz to find out whether you're a born BS detector or the butt of everyone's practical jokes.

1. Are you a decent liar?

a. No, I'm terrible at it.
b. I'm okay. Sometimes I can pull it off.
c. Yes, sometimes I even do it just for fun.

2. Have you ever been the victim of an April Fool's joke?

a. Every year.
b. Sure—but I've always gotten my friends back.
c. I don't fall for them, I plan them.

3. A radio station calls and says you won a car. You say:

a. "Cool! What kind?"
b. "Ummm...okay. How'd that happen?"
c. "Who is this?"

4. When did you stop believing in the tooth fairy?

a. You mean there's no tooth fairy?!
b. Between the ages of 6 and 12 years old.
c. Under 6 years old.

5. How many times have you forwarded a chain e-mail?

a. Tons of times—and where's my money?
b. A few times, but then I realized they're hoaxes.
c. Once—all the way to my "delete" box.

6. A guy doesn't call after he says he will. You think:

a. He must have a girlfriend or else he lost my number.
b. He's too nervous or too busy to call.
c. He never meant to call in the first place.

Add 'em up!

Give yourself 1 point for each a, 2 for each b, and 3 for each c.

6–9 points: Easily fooled

You're so trusting that you take everything at face value. That's a nice thing, because it means you always look for the good in everyone. But it could get you in trouble, because people might find that you're a good target for little pranks. You don't have to be the fall guy, though: Just be a little more suspicious when things sound too good to be true—it often means they are.

10–14 points: Radar-ready gullible? Not really.

But you're not a cynic, either. You like trusting people and giving them the benefit of the doubt, but you're good at knowing when someone's trying to pull one over on you. You've got an exceptionally balanced ability to figure out when something isn't quite right, but to also accept things as they are whenever you can. Good for you, smarty!

15–18 points: Super-cynical

You look at everything with a detective's eye for suspicious details. And while it's good not to believe everything you hear, you might be second-guessing things for no good reason. Try to put some trust in people—you'll find you have more energy left to enjoy life when you're not always scrutinizing it. Trust us.

hear me roar

WHO RUNS YOUR LIFE?

Find out if your friends' opinions really matter.

1. You think the new guy in your math class is hot, but your friend says he looks like a loser. You:

a. Think, "To each her own" and then start coming up with ways to ask him out.

b. Wait a few days until you can figure out for yourself whether he's a stud or a dud.

c. Start to reconsider your crush—maybe she has a point and he's not that great.

2. Your friends are raving about the latest Zac Efron flick. You hated it. When they ask you what you thought, you say:

a. "It sucked. I want those hours back!"

b. "It was okay—but not Zac's best movie. Then again, I'm no Ebert."

c. "It was pretty good. Think about it; anything with Zac in it can't be that bad."

3. You want to audition for the school play, but your friends are trying to talk you out of it since none of them think it's cool. You:

a. Take the stage without them. You're more determined than ever to snag a role and get to know the theater girls.

b. Do your best to persuade one of your closest friends to audition with you.

c. Stick to things your friends do—maybe next year you'll audition.

4. Your curfew is an hour earlier than everyone else's. You:

a. Try to have as much fun as you possibly can with your friends before you head home on time.

b. Do your best to convince your parents that you deserve that extra sixty minutes of freedom because all your friends have it.

c. Stay out the extra hour anyway and use an excuse that one of your friends comes up with.

5. You find out that your lab partner stole the answer key to next week's big biology exam. You:

a. Immediately tell her to trash it—if your teacher questions the class, you will not risk your grade by flat-out lying for her.
b. Do not look at it and try to persuade her to get rid of it before she gets caught.
c. Celebrate your good fortune by treating her to lunch at Taco Bell.

6. After trying on a million bikinis, you find one that you think looks great. Then your shopping buddy says, "You're not going to buy that, are you?" In return, you say:

a. "Not only am I going to buy it—I'm planning on wearing it until it falls apart!"
b. "Why? What's wrong with it? I actually thought it was pretty flattering."
c. "No way! I was just joking! Ha-ha."

7. You're at a party and your favorite can't-help-but-shake-your-groove-thang song comes on. No one is dancing, so you:

a. Get up and bust a move anyway. Once everyone sees how much fun you're having, chances are they'll join in.
b. Grab your least rhythmically challenged friend by the hand and do everything you can to get her to dance with you.
c. Stay put and start tapping your foot—your friends would mock you for the rest of your life if you danced alone.

Scoring

mostly a's: Ms. Independent

The coolest thing about you is that you're not afraid to voice your opinion or try things that others might not. If you like the music, then you'll dance—no matter what all the other wallflowers are doing! Stick to your guns, girl! Your fierce adventurous streak sets you up for opportunities that followers might let pass them by—like the lead role in the school play!

mostly b's: Thorough Thinker

You respect your friends' opinions—but you won't follow advice that you don't agree with. Like with the curfew rule, for instance: You'd never make your parents mad just to make your friends happy. So sometimes you fall in with the crowd, and other times you go solo. Either way, your friends give you props for respecting their right to express themselves—and they respect you even more for knowing when to disagree.

mostly c's: Always Eager to Please

Your friends mean the world to you. You value their opinions—and usually you're willing to do just about anything for them. But when you ignore your this-isn't-right-for-me radar, you're much more likely to fall into sketchy—or downright dangerous—situations, like getting caught with the stolen exam. So don't be afraid to stand up for what you believe in—friends worth keeping will admire you all the more.

DO YOUR OWN THING

Want to stand your ground? Here's how:

- Recognize the real deal. Only fake friends would ditch you just because of a different point of view—true friends appreciate your unique beliefs. Don't freak out—speak out.

- If you have a different opinion, try to be calm and clear instead of rude or mean.

- Practice being all ears. A plan isn't necessarily bad just because someone else came up with it—so always listen up before deciding what to do.

WHAT'S YOUR FIGHTING STYLE?

When a battle brews, do you stand your ground or suffer in silence?

1. Your best bud borrowed—and lost—your new sunglasses. You . . .

a. Don't say anything, but vow to yourself that you'll think twice before letting her borrow anything of yours ever again.
b. Tell her you're upset, but accept her apology and let her buy you a CD.
c. Spread the word to all of your other friends that she totally can't be trusted.

2. You show up at a friend's house at 6 o'clock sharp, but she swears you said you'd be there at 5. It's now 7 p.m. and she's still ranting. You . . .

a. Apologize (again!). Even though it was a simple misunderstanding, you really hate it when she's mad at you.

b. Tell her to get over it already and that pouting won't turn back the clock.
c. Say that you've had enough, split, and don't return her calls for three days.

3. Your new job at the juice bar comes with one little problem: Your coworker expects you to give free smoothies to all her friends. You . . .

a. Become a giveaway queen. Who wants to deal with a scary confrontation?
b. Tell her (nicely) that you don't feel comfortable with the freebiefest.
c. Say—loud enough for the manager to hear—"Um, your friend forgot to pay" the next time she offers up a free one.

4. Ever since you confessed to a friend about your crush, she hasn't stopped hanging all over him. You let her know you're peeved by . . .

a. Giving her the silent treatment for a few days. She'll figure out why you're so annoyed with her sooner or later.

b. Asking her flat-out why she's suddenly become his new close friend.

c. Threatening to tell him about her alcoholic dad if she doesn't back off.

5. You fork over a twenty for your combo meal deal, but the cashier only gives you change for a ten. You . . .

a. Assume you were the one who counted wrong and just let it go.

b. Calmly but firmly point out the error and speak with a manager if you need to.

c. Make a scene and tell everyone around that the cashier is a thief and a liar. You want her to be very sorry for her mistake.

6. Your crush finally calls, but your sister erases the message before you hear it. When you call her on it, she's not exactly apologetic. You . . .

a. Stomp to your room and fantasize about getting back at her (though you know you won't actually do anything).

b. Tell her point-blank that you've been waiting all week for his call and you're really angry that she erased it.

c. Declare war and erase every one of her messages for the next two weeks.

7. You've been waiting in line all night for concert tickets when the group in front of you lets yet another bunch of their friends cut in front of them. You . . .

a. Try to catch the eye of the mean-looking guy behind you and hope he's p.o.'d too so he'll kick them out of line.

b. Point out to the cutters that the end of the line is around the corner.

c. Get them booted by yelling "Security! These guys are letting people cut!"

Scoring

Give yourself 1 point for every a, 2 for every b, and 3 for every c.

17 to 21 points: Warrior Princess

You're emotional, and you fight to win—even if it means fighting dirty. The next time you get into an argument, take a deep breath and listen to what your "opponent" has to say before blasting into her. After all, what good is winning a fight if you lose a friend (or maybe several)?

12 to 16 points: Fair Fighter

You keep yourself composed but you're not afraid to express your true feelings—and the facts. Even when someone hits below the belt, you respond calmly and rationally. And because you almost never lose your cool, your friends aren't afraid to tell you when you've done something that really bugged them.

7 to 11 points: Denial Queen

Even when you know you should stand your ground, you hate rocking the boat. The next time someone makes you mad, think about exactly what you want to say to that person—then say it! Holding your feelings in will stress you out more, and it could make you resent other people. If you speak up when you're upset—without losing control—friends will respect you, and they might even apologize.

WAGE A WINNING BATTLE

You'll more likely get your way if you:

● Stick to the subject. If you say mean things about unrelated issues (like "No wonder your boyfriend cheated on you..."), you'll regret it later.

● Avoid absolutes. If you say something like, "You never listen to me," you're just setting yourself up to be proven wrong— of course your mom listens to you some of the time!

● Hear her out. Your opponent needs to know you're listening and not just thinking about your next comeback. So wait until she's finished and then say "I can see your point, but . . ."

ARE YOU A GOAL GETTER?

Do you control your life, or does it control you?

1. You have a math test, a paper on the Civil War, and an art project all due the same day. You . . .

a. Panic. You'll study for the test and beg your other teachers for an extension.

b. Prioritize. You'll just block off separate times for each assignment.

c. Procrastinate. You'll load up on candy and caffeine the night before and cram. That's how you work best, anyway.

2. That adorable skater guy you have a crush on smiles at you in the hall. You . . .

a. Go to his favorite ramp every day to see him skate (homework, be darned!).

b. Find out his class schedule and "coincidentally" bump into him before lunch.

c. Ask him what he's up to Saturday and make plans to hang out—even if your whole weekend is already booked.

3. You're dying to go on a trip with a friend's family, but your mom and dad won't pay. So you . . .

a. Get a waitressing job. If the tips are lousy, you'll work six shifts a week (even if you have to quit the play).

b. Get a weekend job. A few Saturdays making lattes should earn you just enough cash.

c. Scrounge up cash doing random chores. It'll add up, right?

4. Your sister's birthday is coming up, and you want to make her a great scrapbook. You'll probably . . .

a. Stay up all night to finish it right away even though you have a huge swim meet the next day.

b. Work on it a little every day for a week so that it's ready in time.

c. Get totally overwhelmed and give it to her a week late.

98

5. The last time you went shopping for a dress for a school dance, you . . .

a. Wanted something very specific and shopped every day for a month until you found it.

b. Found a great dress that went well with your favorite pair of evening shoes.

c. Store-hopped for six hours and blew your cash on dirty denim jeans instead.

6. Your mom's tired of buying Halloween costumes, so you offer to make one for your little brother. At 3 p.m., October 31, you're . . .

a. Arguing with your mom. (She's annoyed you spent more money on the supplies than if you'd just bought the costume.)

b. Finishing up your brother's face paint and sending him out the door.

c. Desperately trying to make something out of an old bedsheet in time.

7. It's class election time, and you've decided to run for student council. Your campaign strategy:

a. Spend every minute campaigning, even if it means less time spent with friends.

b. Ask a friend to be campaign manager; the two of you can get all the poster and button making done on weekends.

c. Well, you had some great ideas but you were too busy to make them happen.

Scoring

mostly a's: Super-focused

You're great at zooming in, but you only focus on one thing at a time. When your mind's set on a goal (like getting a part in the school play or acing a history test), you go too far and either drop everything else in your life or veer away from the original plan. Spread out your super-honing skills by taking on a few projects at once and setting small daily goals. You'll see you really can do it all. Promise.

mostly b's: Great goalie

You're great at planning ahead and meeting your goals—whether they're serious (like school) or fun (like making time for friends). Being able to juggle multiple tasks will always help you stay on track—just be sure to plan for some downtime too. Read a book or rent a movie with friends—you'll de-stress and be able to meet your goals even better.

mostly c's: Juggling act

You're great at starting projects, but finishing them is another story. You just have too many other exciting things going on at once. If you're tempted to drop something halfway through, focus on getting through to the end. Then reward yourself! Limit yourself to just a few projects at once, and then map out a way to meet your goals. P.S.: If you don't own a planner, get one now!

TOTAL TASKMASTER

To stay on top of your to-dos . . .

- Be a clock wizard. Time every task for a week (from reading a chapter of history to washing the dishes). Then use that info to help you plan in the future.
- Make a "time map." Color code your planner with blocks of time (red for school, blue for friends, etc.).
- Just say no. Before you take on a new project, ask yourself: How will this help me? If you don't know, let it go.

ARE YOU A LEADER?

Find out if your friends look up to you—or look back to make sure you're there.

1. You and your girls are planning a surprise birthday party for a friend. You immediately:

a. Start organizing who's going to take care of invitations, gifts, decorations, snacks, etc.

b. Say, "Does anyone mind if I play DJ? I have a couple of really good mixes in mind."

c. Go, "Let me know what I need to do"—and then do what they tell you.

2. Your group wants to give old clothes to Goodwill, but no one's sure how to get them there. You:

a. Figure out a day that's convenient to stop by each one's house so you can fill your trunk and get it done in one big haul.

b. Offer to drop it all off—if they'll just bring what they have to your house.

c. Wait for someone else to figure out what you guys need to do.

3. You're in the hall when a new girl trips and drops her books all over the place. You:

a. Smile at her, walk over, and help her pull her stuff together.

b. Smile sympathetically but help her only if someone else does first!

c. Think, She must be so embarrassed.

4. On the first day of driver's ed, your teacher asks the class to introduce themselves. You:

a. Raise your hand and say, "I'm Jen, and I'm here to learn to drive stick."

b. Make eye contact and smile at her so she knows that if she needs a volunteer, you're willing to go first.

c. Look down and hope that someone else in the class speaks up soon.

5. One friend of yours always makes plans but then doesn't show up. You deal with it by:

a. Saying you feel like she's been blowing you off lately and asking her to be more considerate.

b. Only inviting her to group activities so her absence won't ruin any plans.

c. Shrugging it off. What can you really do about it anyway?

6. At the movies, some friends want to see a comedy while the rest are big on a drama. You say:

a. "I'd rather watch the comedy later on video—I'll see the drama if anyone wants to come with."

b. "Why don't we take a vote? Or we could just split up and all meet after and do something."

c. "Really, I'm fine with either."

7. Two friends tell you and another friend that they're ditching class to go shopping. You:

a. Say, "No thanks—I don't want to have to play catch-up later."

b. Say, "Maybe next time. I have a quiz today"—even if you don't.

c. Do whatever your friend decides to.

Scoring

Give yourself 1 point for every a, 2 for every b, and 3 for every c. Now add 'em up!

7–11 points: First Lady

Your friends think you're a bold girl, but the real word for you is leader! You're not freaked by being first, because you see the big picture. Instead of "What will they think of me?" you ask, "How can I help make this happen?" So take your talents beyond just your social circle. Apply them to a school or community group, and we'll see you at the top!

12–16 points: Independent Woman

If others are more impassioned about something than you are, you'll step back, but if you have a strong opinion, you're not afraid to speak up. To become a better leader, study a friend who does it well. How does she approach people? How does she balance her opinion with others'? Use her lessons in your life, and you'll be team captain soon too!

17–21 points: Group Thinker

Your friends love that you're always willing to join in on their plans. The only problemo? You may do things you don't want to—just to get along with others. Next time you think, I wish we were doing this instead, say it! You might be outvoted, but either way, saying what's on your mind earns you respect.

Discover Your Personality

get to
know yourself

WHO ARE YOU?

Take this quiz and you can uncover the hidden powers of your personality!

Pick your answers: For each statement, give yourself 4 points for the answer that fits you best, 3 points for the next best, 2 for the third best, and 1 for the one that fits you least. (Don't worry—there are no "right" answers!)

1. In school, you enjoy:
a. History/civics.
b. Phys ed.
c. English/writing.
d. Science/math.

2. In your family, your role is the:
a. Helping hand.
b. Troublemaker.
c. Peacekeeper.
d. Voice of reason.

3. You're drawn to a guy who is:
a. Dependable and level headed.
b. Bold and free-spirited.
c. Sensitive and soulful.
d. Smart and independent.

4. Your most typical mood is:
a. Cautious and responsible.
b. Excited and stimulated.
c. Eager and motivated.
d. Calm and detached.

5. You most want to have:
a. Security.
b. Fun.
c. Self-understanding.
d. Knowledge.

6. You pride yourself on your:
a. Good judgment.
b. Creativity.
c. Ambition.
d. Competence.

7. You want to become a:
a. Good citizen.
b. Big star.
c. Well-rounded person.
d. Great genius.

8. You want others to see you as:
a. Hardworking.
b. Playful.
c. Sincere.
d. Strong-willed.

Scoring

Are you a guardian, an artisan, an idealist, or a realist? Discover your secret personality traits—and the incredible power they give you. Just add up all the *a*'s, the *b*'s, the *c*'s, and the *d*'s. Whichever letter has the highest score holds the key to uncovering your true self. Use that power to be the best you can be!

If a was your highest score . . . Guardian

Guardians are sensible, down-to-earth people who value family and give back to their community. Others depend on you to get the job done because you understand how to play by the rules—and win.

If b was your highest score . . . Artisan

Artisans are impulsive, sensual people who want to be free to do what they want, how they want. You never take no for an answer. Instead, you don't rest until you figure out how to accomplish your goals (which you always do).

If c was your highest score . . . Idealist

Idealists are imaginative, enthusiastic, ethical people who constantly analyze themselves to discover who they are. You're continually striving for self-improvement, and you never act phony and always stand by your beliefs—no matter what the risk.

If d was your highest score . . . Realist

Realists are curious, skeptical, and fiercely independent thinkers. You want to understand how things work so you can make them work even better. Instead of relying on what's already there, you push yourself until you come up with new and innovative ideas.

DISCOVER YOUR SECRET SELF!

See how the colors you choose instantly reveal the real you!

Did you know that your color preferences reveal your personality traits, like what motivates you? So clear your head and pick the first color you're drawn to. Don't think about how great you look in red—it's about your gut reaction to the colors. Choose one from the left set of colored rings below, then one from the right. Now find the analysis for your color combo on page 115 and let the Dewey Color System show you what you're *really* all about.

PICK ONE OF THESE

PICK ONE OF THESE

Your true colors: Find your combination below and get ready to meet your inner self!

red–green
You're Miss Practical—and nothing can shake your levelheadedness. Your calm demeanor helps to keep everyone around you sane.

yellow–green
Caretaking comes naturally to you, and you feel fulfilled by it. You're the one friends always come to when they need support and a ready ear.

blue–green
Your curiosity motivates you, and you're extremely observant. You can see people's dreams and give them the self-confidence to follow through.

red–purple
Order is your middle name. You're at your best when in control or directing others, which is probably why you plan all those super events!

yellow–purple
Change fuels your inner fire, and you live to be on the go, exploring new places. Each new adventure brings you a stronger sense of self.

blue–purple
You're always the center of attention, and people are drawn to you. You're inspired to turn grandiose daydreams into amazing realities.

red–orange
You thrive on individuality—and never follow the crowd. You're a take-action girl who fights for those who can't express themselves as freely.

yellow–orange
You are a constant innovator who loves making something out of nothing. You're always seeking out challenges to avoid getting stuck in a rut.

blue–orange
One minute you're creative and free, the next you're all logic. This duality keeps everyone on their toes, which makes you the life of any party.

ARE YOU AN IT GIRL?

Pssst! There's a new girl who's stepping into the spotlight. Could she be you? Take this quick quiz to find out!

Answer true or false to each statement below, then tally your score to see if you put the *isma* in *charisma*!

1. My friends frequently come to me seeking my advice for their problems.
   TRUE ✓
   FALSE ___

2. When I meet new people, my mind doesn't wander off. I'm usually really interested.
   TRUE ✓
   FALSE ___

3. I try to put people at ease. It doesn't matter who they are—I think it's best when people are comfortable around me.
   TRUE ✓
   FALSE ___

4. I get excited about many of the same things that excite my friends.
   TRUE ✓
   FALSE ___

5. I can find something to like about almost everyone I meet, even if it's a little thing.
   TRUE ___
   FALSE ✓

6. I don't worry a lot about the impression that I make on other people. I'm pretty confident that I give off a good vibe.
   TRUE ✓
   FALSE ✓

7. People notice that I'm usually in high spirits.
   TRUE ✓
   FALSE ___

8. The way I see it, most people have a lot to say—and I'm happy to hear it.

TRUE ____
FALSE ✓

9. Most of my friends would be surprised to find that I have problems just like theirs.

TRUE ____
FALSE ✓

TRUE ✓
FALSE ____

10. I like it when people share with me the little details of their lives. It's what makes them interesting and unique!

Give yourself one point for every time you answered TRUE.

TOTAL 8

How Many Points Did You Score?

8–10 points: You've got it

People gravitate toward you because you have that gift of making them feel at ease. That's why you have tons of friends!

5–7 points: You're working on it

You know how to tune in to others' good qualities, so make an effort to show off *yours*, and you're sure to become It.

1–4 points: You could use more of it

You're an amazing person—so let people in on the secret!
Hint: Try starting a conversation by complimenting someone. It works!

Girls with the most charisma would answer true to every question. Here's why:

(1) A charismatic person is a nonjudgmental confidant—
her friends trust her.

(2) She pays attention to people and

(3) cares about making them feel relaxed around her.

(4) She's enthusiastic about the things that make her friends feel good,

(5) is friendly and outgoing,

(6) and acts self-assured by not obsessing about what others think of her.

(7) She's upbeat and positive, and

(8) enjoys conversation.

(9) She seems worry-free, even though she has issues like everyone else.

(10) People can talk to her about anything—she's genuinely interested in others' stories.

DISCOVER YOUR INNER GODDESS

Thought mythology was boring?
Take our quiz and think again!

Directions and scoring: Read each pair of statements and choose the one that describes you best.

1.
a. I think that I'm more of a dreamer than practical.
b. I think that I'm more practical than a dreamer.

2.
a. I like variety in life more than a regular routine.
b. I prefer to stick with things I already know how to do.

3.
a. I think most issues have many different sides.
b. Most issues have two sides—a right and a wrong one.

4.
a. I love to think up new ways to do things.
b. I like to do things the way they've always worked.

5.
c. I'm the type who analyzes situations and problems.
d. I'm more of a "doer" than a "thinker."

6.
c. My head usually rules my heart.
d. I make decisions based mostly on my feelings.

7.
c. I always do more work than what's asked of me.
d. I do just enough work to get by.

8.
c. I'd rather compete than collaborate as a group.
d. I'd rather collaborate than compete.

Scoring

Add up how many a's, b's, c's, and d's you picked. The two most common letters in your results will reveal your goddess sister, below.

a+c Artemis

Just like Artemis, you're a natural-born leader who hits whatever target you aim for. You're as brave as they come and are always willing to fight for what you believe in. Being a leader comes easy for you because you see the big picture and aren't afraid to make tough decisions. But sometimes you do forget to include others in your plans or to get their support, so try to remember that the people around you are there to help—and they probably have great ideas too!

a+d Psyche

The most mystical of goddesses, Psyche continually searches for insight and purpose in her life, and so do you. It's that curiosity, creativity, and sense of wonder that help you to keep growing as a person. And because you're so sensitive to what's going on around you, you easily pick up on other people's moods and provide a great shoulder to cry on. But trying to help everyone out all the time can get overwhelming, so find time to focus on your needs and pamper yourself once in a while.

b+c Athena

You, Athena girl, are wise beyond your years! With your knowledge and strong desire to succeed, you master whatever you set out to do. It may take longer than you'd like, since you carefully think things through, but it always gets done—thanks to your steady determination. Just be careful: Your combination of drive and logic can lead you to believe you're always right. Try to take other people's feelings into consideration before you automatically dismiss their ideas.

b+d Aphrodite

As an Aphrodite girl, you shine in the spotlight and always have admirers. That's because you take advantage of all that life has to offer by living in the moment, trying new things, and making sure everyone around you is having fun too. But when things get gloomy, you tend to take off for brighter surroundings. Instead of running away, make an effort to deal with any unpleasantness head on—once you actively try to work it out, you'll see how strong and capable you really are!

DO PEOPLE GET YOU?

Find out if you're a good communicator— and how to become one if you're not!

1. When a friend asks you to lie to her mom on her behalf, it makes you uncomfortable, so you:

a. Say, "Uh, um...yeah, sure. Whatever."

b. Say, "Okay" but let your phone go to voice mail when her mom actually calls.

c. Say, "I'm not comfortable doing that."

2. Your mom asks you to describe the dress you fell in love with at the mall. You say:

a. "It was, like, pink with, like, a black satin, ya know, bow around the waist."

b. "It was pink with, like, a black satin bow around the waist."

c. "It was pink with a black satin bow around the waist."

3. A close friend said she'd call you back, but she didn't. When you see her in school the next day:

a. You pretend like everything's fine, even though you're sort of hurt.

b. You give her one-word answers so she'll get the hint and ask if you're mad.

c. You say, "You never called me back last night. What happened?"

4. Now that you think about it, who's doing most of the talking in your everyday conversations?

a. You; your friends and family actually tease you about your *loooong* stories.

b. The other person; you respond, but you're not much of a conversation starter.

c. It's balanced; you and the other person both talk— and listen.

5. You don't want to cover your coworker's shift when your boss asks if you're able to, so you say:

a. "If you really need me, I guess I can."
b. "I actually already made other plans that I can't get out of."
c. "I'm sorry, but I can't that day."

6. You're talking to your teacher about an assignment. What is your body language like?

a. You have your arms crossed.
b. You're waving your hands around to drive home the point you're making.
c. You're leaning in toward her.

7. You're talking to your crush, and you disagree with something he says about animal rights.
You:

a. Act like you agree so he won't think you're argumentative or something.
b. Casually change the topic and hope he doesn't bring it up again.
c. Tell him that you see his point, but you think [your opinion here!].

8. When your teacher calls on you in class, are you able to look her in the eye?

a. No, not really.
b. Sometimes.
c. Yeah. Why wouldn't I be?

Scoring

a. Well, uh, no

You're not clear with people about what you want or think. Each time you hold yourself back from saying what you mean, write down how you *wish* you'd handled the situation. Then you can try to do *that* the next time!

b. Sort of . . . sometimes

When you're comfortable, you're clear. But if you're intimidated, you get tongue-tied. Next time you feel awkward saying what you think, force yourself to *speak up*. It may feel unnatural, but you'll build the skill—and your confidence.

c. Definitely yes

Your directness will help you forge solid relationships now and in the future! Be sure that you also let others say what they need to—and that you *think* about their point before responding. That way, you'll get them as much as they get you!

ARE YOU A STRESS CASE?

Midterm! Crush! Curfew! Okay, take five minutes out of your life for this quiz— you may need it more than you know.

Add up the points of every statement that applies to your life over the past six months.

1. You got your driver's license (yahoo!) and started driving on your own.
(20 points) ___✓___

2. You often feel guilty or nervous about something.
(25 points) ___✓___

3. You have unexplained stomachaches or headaches at least twice a week.
(25 points each) ___✓___

4. You tend to blush or sweat more than usual in social situations.
(25 points) ___✓___

5. You have a harder time sleeping than normal or have a lot of nightmares.
(25 points) ___✓___

6. Your looks have changed (not just a haircut—more like a big change in weight).
(30 points) ___✓___

7. You've gotten into a new relationship or ended one you had.
(35 points) ___✓___

8. You applied to college (or you're in the process of applying right now).
(40 points) _____

9. You've had lots of problems with your grades or with one particular teacher.
(45 points) ✓

10. You're taking Advanced Placement or honors classes.
(45 points) _____

11. You do after-school activities that take up at least 10 hours a week.
(45 points) _____

12. You and your family have moved to a different city.
(65 points) _____

13. A new baby brother or sister has entered your family.
(70 points) _____

14. Your parents got divorced or decided to separate.
(80 points) _____

15. You got pregnant without wanting to or meaning to.
(80 points) _____

16. A parent **(100 points)**, sibling **(95 points)**, or best friend **(90 points)** died. _____

Scoring

over 200 points: High

You're under a lot of stress, but try not to feel hopeless. Stress is about how in-control you feel. So, put your stresses into two lists: "things I can change" (college stress) and "things I can't" (your parents' divorce). Take charge of the "can't" list by talking to a counselor (even *asking* for help puts you in control). And for the "can" list, make a de-stressing plan. Maybe map out a college application schedule to break up the process into manageable chunks (college visits, essay due dates).

100–200 points: Medium

You are definitely stressed, whether it's because of a major life-changing event or just a hectic schedule. You need to stop and smell the mocha latte, and make downtime a *priority*. Here's how: Schedule two hours each week in your planner for something relaxing. Some people like physical stuff, like running, but you could also bake cookies or even read romance novels—whatever calms you. And the next time anyone asks you to take on a stressful task, tell them your schedule's *full*.

under 100 points: Low

You're in control, girl. You've been lucky not to have been through many earth-shattering events lately, and if little stuff's come up, you've dealt and avoided stress symptoms. That'll make you healthier for *life*. You're in such good shape, you could benefit from challenging yourself. Think of something scary you've wanted to do (like running for class office), and let that stress motivate you to take the risk. What feels like fear might *actually* be your inner spirit chanting, "Go for it!"

WHAT'S YOUR SECRET STRENGTH?

*You have a superpower. Oh, yes you do!
Now, find it!*

1. When you get older, you'll be:

a. An actor.
b. A detective.
c. An ad exec.
d. A firefighter.

2. If you were a pair of shoes you'd be:

a. Simple black flats.
b. Puma-esque sneakers.
c. Black stiletto boots.
d. Red leather platforms.

3. Your crush has a crush on someone else. You:

a. Find a *new* crush.
b. Cry a little, then gracefully accept defeat.
c. Trust your gut and wait it out—he'll come around.
d. Fight for him.

4. Next to your bed is the following reading material:

a. The latest best-selling paperback novel.
b. A college pamphlet.
c. An astrology guide.
d. A thick classic, like *Crime and Punishment*.

5. When you meet someone new, you:

a. Talk about the news or latest celeb gossip.
b. Make small talk.
c. Immediatley try to figure that person out.
d. Go around the room introducing her to new people.

6. It's fourth quarter and you're down by one point. You:

a. Are the only one playing who's not nervous.
b. Think, it's just a game.
c. Pray.
d. Go for a game-winning shot if you're open.

Scoring

If you get a tie, you have dual powers. ✗

mostly a's: Versatility

You have the special ability to adapt to any situation. Hardly anything fazes you, because you're so good at thinking on your feet. So whether it's a party, the classroom, a football game, or a debate, you feel right at home—and in control.

mostly b's: X-ray Vision

You are a realist—you see things as they truly are. Your ability to decipher everything you see helps you make smart decisions and keeps you from getting hurt, because you know the drill.

mostly c's: Intuition

You get a vibe, and you go with it. Your instinct helps you in every kind of situation, like knowing the trends before they're cool, winning over teachers, and knowing when that cute guy has a crush on you.

mostly d's: Courage

Wow, Supergirl! There's nothing you're afraid of, and people rely on you because of your mental toughness. Sure, you've been through a few hard times, but there's nothing you can't handle now—and that makes you an inspiration to everyone around you.

ARE YOU HIGH MAINTENANCE?

Find out if you're a pain in the tush or totally laid-back.

1. It's raining! You:

a. Find the biggest puddle to jump in.
b. Pull out your trusty umbrella.
c. Run for the nearest Starbucks.
d. Scream and immediately head home—your hair and makeup are ruined, and now your day is too!

2. If you break a nail, you:

a. Nails? What nails? You bit them off and spit them out yesterday.
b. File it down—the natural look is in!
c. Walk into the nearest salon for an emergency appointment.
d. Page your on-call manicurist.

3. At a party, you:

a. Just drink the store-brand soda.
b. Grab a Coke from the fridge.
c. Ask the cutest guy around to get you a glass of punch.
d. Order the hostess to fetch you a Perrier—and make it snappy!

4. Dressing up for you is:

a. A denim jacket and track pants.
b. Jeans and a sequined tank.
c. Your favorite sexy top and low-slung slim pants.
d. A little black dress, heels, and a blow-out at the salon.

5. If you had to pick one, you'd say your star style is probably closest to:

a. Nelly Furtado.
b. Pink.
c. Beyoncé Knowles.
d. Christina Aguilera.

6. You catch your archrival talking to your crush. You:

a. Let 'em talk—she can have him.
b. Join the conversation.
c. Tell him that you need to talk.
d. Throw a drink in her face and tell her to stay away from your man.

135

Scoring

1 point for every a, 2 for b's, 3 for c's, and 4 for d's.

6-10 points: Death Before Divahood

You're the type of girl who's comfortable rolling out of bed and just living life (ahh!). But beware: You're so content that other, more diva-ish types could try to take advantage of you. So don't you dare let other people be the boss of you, okay?

11-15 points: 99.44% Non-Diva

You know how to happily roll with the punches. You're comfortable being yourself and even know how to compromise with the people around you. But you're nobody's doormat, either.

16-19 points: Being Considered for Divahood

You're über-confident, so it makes sense that you like to do things your way. Independent thinking is great, but so is respecting and appreciating other people's brilliance. Sit back and let your friends have a say sometimes too!

20-24 points: Doyenne of Divas

You want to be your best, and you won't stop until you are. That makes you driven—but some people see it as pushy. So try not to pop a blood vessel when things don't go your way. Instead of throwing a tantrum, try to see the humor in the situation.

ARE YOU TOO SUPERFICIAL?

Look a little bit closer and see for yourself just how image-conscious you really are!

1. A hairdresser gives your friend an awful cut. You:

a. Say, "It looks fine—and it'll grow."
b. Suggest she invest in a cool hat.
c. Make fun of her behind her back.

2. Your nana offers you her brown 1980 Chevy. You:

a. Are psyched to have your own car.
b. Spend your b-day money on a paint job.
c. Say, "Thanks, but no thanks."

3. Your yearbook photo is totally hideous. You:

a. Get bummed but think, Does *anyone* look good in them?
b. Retake pictures to get a better shot.
c. Get airbrushed.

4. You oversleep for school, so you:

a. Skip your shower to arrive on time.
b. Shower, pull your hair back, and arrive 15 minutes late.
c. Skip class so you can get fully ready.

5. You would never date a guy who:

a. Was obnoxious to your friends.
b. Had less-than-popular friends.
c. Didn't dress like Ashton and/or drive a nice car.

6. You work out at the gym so that you can:

a. Get that natural endorphin high.
b. Be part of the whole gym "scene."
c. Look hot in tight jeans and shirts.

When it comes to looks, you . . .

mostly a's: Don't care

Spend time primping and preening? No way! You see beyond the external and think that *character* matters more than looks. But most of the world, alas, does base judgments on what they see. So sometimes—like on interviews—you'll have to take some extra care to look as confident as you feel.

mostly b's: Kinda care

Sure, you'll take a second glance in the mirror. But you also know where to draw the line, and you don't obsess over the way you—or others—look. Keep putting that extra effort into looking good if it helps you *feel* good and gives you a confidence boost, but don't let yourself get carried away.

mostly c's: Care a lot

Put that mirror down! It's fine to look your best on the outside—if you feel as good on the *inside.* If you don't, focus on things you're good at (tennis? cooking?) to remind yourself that you've got substance! And remember: You'll miss out on a lot if you judge people based only on their looks.

HOW MATURE ARE YOU?

Are you wise beyond your years, or are you just a wise-butt?

1. Your parents leave town for the weekend. So you:

a. Throw a huge party and try to make sure nothing gets broken.
b. Get a group of friends together for a last-minute sleepover.
c. Invite a friend over for a movie.
d. Clean the house and water the plants, just like they asked.

2. When you like a guy, how do you usually let him know it? You:

a. Have your best friend tell him.
b. Play hard to get and ignore him.
c. Try to go to his favorite places and "bump into him" a lot.
d. Get to know him first, and let the relationship slowly evolve.

3. You get $100 for your birthday from rich Aunt Janie (wa-ha-hooey!). You:

a. Spend it on shoes.
b. Treat your best friends to dinner—sushi for four, please!
c. Buy a hot new perfume, then save the rest for a rainy day.
d. Save up for a new CD burner.

4. If you were caught in class without your homework, you would:

a. Concoct an elaborate lie about how your bag was stolen.
b. Stall by saying you left it in your locker, then do it at lunch.
c. Explain why you didn't finish it.
d. You *always* do your homework!

5. What do you do if you're going to miss your curfew?

a. Stay out—if you're already in trouble, you may as well live it up.
b. Go home in an hour, but prepare to face consequences.
c. Just get home *fast*—calling might make it into a bigger issue.
d. Call home and explain.

6. Your idea of a perfect after-school job would be:

a. Babysitting, mowing lawns—any hourly job that gives you freedom.
b. Waitressing—the flexible schedule lets you have a life.
c. A retail job (discount alert!).
d. An internship with your own computer and voice mail!

Scoring

Add 1 point for each a, 2 for b's, 3 for c's, and 4 for d's.

6-11 points: Baby Face

"Hello, NBC? We've got a new sitcom for you. It's based on the life of this funny, mischievous girl." Um, that'd be you. But while the outrageous situations you get into would be great on TV, they can make *real* life tough. So, go ahead and act like a kid—just be responsible enough to learn from your mistakes.

12-19 points: Present Perfect

You're responsible enough to know who you are and where you're going (no, not like Arby's—like college!), but there's still a side of you that appreciates Pop-Tarts and old friends. And that's why people love you—you act your (appropriate) age!

20-24 points: Going on 30

Let's see . . . your parents trust you, your friends love your advice, and your teachers consider you a godsend. Yup, you've got it together! Have you ever noticed how people call you an "old soul"? But don't forget to play in the sprinklers sometimes—when life gets serous, know how to have fun!

143

ARE YOU WEIRD?

Learn to love your inner freakazoid . . .
We know she's in there somewhere.

1. Your new teacher asks everyone about their hobbies. You knit, run, and watch lots of movies. You say:

a. "I watch foreign movies no one's heard of—like *Audition,* where this girl cuts off this guy's leg and puts all these needles in his eyes."

b. "I run cross-country, and, oh, I also like to knit sometimes."

c. "I like to go jogging."

2. You're eating breakfast on the go, and you wind up spilling grape juice all over your top, so you:

a. Wear it like that and tell everyone you got into a horrible accident with Grimace in the parking lot of McDonald's on your way to school.

b. Cover it up with your skater friend's tee. (He always wears at least two.)

c. Change into the spare shirt you keep in your locker *at all times.*

3. Your assignment: Do an in-class presentation on Shirley Temple. Naturally, you:

a. Wear a totally outrageous polka-dot dress, put your hair in tight curls, and tap-dance.

b. Show some key movie clips, and bring in Sprite and grenadine to serve the drink named after her.

c. Give a moving speech about her life, from her child-star days to her job with the State Department.

4. Which of the following makeup products would you be most likely to impulse-buy?

a. Turquoise rainbow-glitter mascara.

b. Super-shiny magenta nail polish.

c. A nice rose lipstick that's just a shade lighter than your lips.

5. During truth or dare, you're dared to "sleepwalk" into your friend's brother's room. You:

a. Barge into his room, add some loud talking and snoring for extra effect, and dramatically bump into things (including him).

b. Slowly open his door, take a few steps in, then run back out.

c. Ask for a truth instead.

6. If you found out you just won the Volkswagen of your choice, you'd ask for:

a. "One of those old vans from the '70s—preferably with a shag carpet."

b. "A Beetle—but in slate gray. None of that wacky bright green for me."

c. "A Jetta."

7. Which celebrity do you look at and go, "You know, when I'm famous, I want to be like *her*"?

a. Gwen Stefani.

b. Drew Barrymore.

c. Mandy Moore.

Scoring

Give yourself 1 point for every a, 2 for every b, and 3 for every c. Now add 'em up!

7–11 points: Truly Bizarro

You know how people say, "You're insane!"? Well, you're not. But you act the way you want to act without worrying what other people think. That's considered weird because most *adults* don't even dare to go their own way. Basically, you're brave. So how can you be more normal? Don't even *try!* As long as you're not getting yourself in trouble, you're being normal . . . for you! Weird on, CosmoGIRL!

12–16 points: Classically Strange

Sure, you might break-dance in the cafeteria, but you save the moves for when the vice principal isn't on lunch duty. When "normal" is needed (i.e., in class or on a job interview), you can play that role, too. As long as neither way of "acting" stresses you out, you're just doing a good job of expressing yourself honestly. Weirdo!

17–21 points: Weirdly Normal

You're the queen of common sense, and we love it. But nobody's perfect, so you might be holding yourself back to seem totally together. Look, it's *okay* to bug out over Burt Bacharach or wear an "odd" tee if it's what you want to do. So when you want to do something offbeat, think, Who cares if I seem "weird"?! Then go for it!

ARE YOU MOTIVATED?

Turbo Girl . . . or Turtle Girl?
Put your zest to the test!

1. *All right!* You get paired with your crush for your English class screenplay project. You . . .

a. Run up to him after class and tell him every detail of your brilliant idea.
b. Tell him you'll start thinking up storylines.
c. Let *him* make the first move. If he writes the whole movie, then he'll *really* be your leading man.

2. The school radio station needs a DJ. When the media teacher asks you to fill the post, you say . . .

a. You'd be *thrilled* to.
b. You'll think about it for a while. (*Four whole* after-school hours?)
c. No way—you'd have to miss *Oprah.*

3. Oh, man—it's two stress-filled days before your make-it-or-break-it biology test. You . . .

a. Memorize the entire skeletal system in a three-hour power session.
b. Crack your book and make an outline.
c. Complain to your friends that you'll never be able to memorize how this bone is connected to that bone.

4. Your best friend's fitness frenzy is rubbing off on you. You . . .

a. Show up at her house in your full jogging gear first thing in the morning.
b. Do fifty sit-ups before bed two nights a week.
c. Put on your Pumas and watch beach aerobics on TV.

5. Your parents warn you: Clean up your bedroom or kiss your phone privileges good-bye. You . . .

a. Morph into a crazy cleaning machine, pronto.

b. Take an MTV break, then pick up the pigsty in time to beat your friend's phone curfew.

c. Tell your folks to keep the cordless: You're not going *near* that disaster area.

6. It's finally Friday—but there's zilch going on for the weekend. You . . .

a. Tell your friends to meet at your house at 7 p.m. sharp—you've planned a surprise spa party!

b. Start making plans to guarantee that *next* weekend is awesome.

c. Sit at home hoping the phone will ring.

7. You're freaking out over paying for your Spring Break beach trip. You decide to . . .

a. Lie about your age and sell your plasma or your unfertilized eggs.

b. Baby-sit every Friday from now till then.

c. Announce to relatives that you'd like to receive money instead of a gift for every holiday (please).

8. You log on and . . . woo-hoo! "You've got mail!" You hit the reply button . . .

a. Immediately. You want to make sure you have more mail tomorrow.

b. For *some* of the messages. You don't bother to answer boring group e-mails.

c. Later. You save your old mail and promise yourself you'll write back someday. Maybe Saturday?

Scoring

20 to 24 points: Miss Motivation

You never have to be nagged—even if the mission is de-molding the refrigerator. For superhuman overachievers like yourself, success is a sure thing. But there's something missing from your bright future: *Sleep!* So, how can you chill out? Schedule some downtime—literally. If "goof off" is on your to-do list, you'll feel better about actually doing it.

14 to 19 points: Break-taker

You're not the type to tune into a *Real World* marathon, but you don't feel the need to do stuff ASAP, either. You get things done, but you're also willing to cut loose and have some fun. Your last-second scrambles can cause excess stress. Allowing extra time for unforeseen snags will cut down on your panic.

8 to 13 points: Serious Slacker

You're not oblivious to the fact that things need to be done; you're just a master at putting stuff off—and off. But there are times when you need to force yourself into just-do-it mode: If you respond to everything with a no-can-do attitude, you'll be missing out on some pretty amazing life experiences.

CAN YOU TELL A GOOD RISK FROM A BAD ONE?

1. Woo-hoo! Your friend invites you, a ski virgin, to hit the slopes. You accept. When you get to Mt. Humongo, the first thing you do is . . .

a. Head for the hardest run. Nothing ventured, nothing gained!

b. Sign up for a lesson. A broken leg is not your idea of a fashion statement.

c. Take a seat by the fire at the lodge. You'll leave the daredevil stuff to your friend, Little Miss Super-Skier.

2. Your prankster friends decide to sneak into the guys' locker room, steal their boxers, and run them up the flagpole. You agree to . . .

a. Plan and execute the maneuver. They call *you* when it's mission impossible.

b. Stand lookout. You want a piece of the fun—without handling the merch.

c. Hear all about it later. You can't get detention for just listening!

3. One of your fellow cashiers at the Food Mart invites you to her New Year's Eve bash, but you won't know a soul there. You say . . .

a. "Par-*tay*! I can't wait to meet all those new cute guys."

b. "Can I bring my three best friends? We travel as a group."

c. "Um, thanks, but I should keep my parents company— we always watch the ball drop on TV."

4. You'll wait on a long line at the amusement park just to get on . . .

a. The ten-story bungee jump— free fall is so excellent!

b. The log flume ride—you like the splash without the crash.

c. The carousel—now that you're older, it doesn't make you dizzy!

5. After seeing Beyoncé in concert, you know you want to be a singer. Your plan of action is to . . .

a. Sign up to sing at open-mike night. Why not go for it?

b. Beg your parents for voice lessons. Your teacher will help you develop your "potential."

c. Sing your heart out in the shower when no one's home—the last thing you need is for your *sister* to make fun of you.

6. The hottest guy you've ever seen is hanging with some people from your class. You . . .

a. March right up, say "hey" to the people you know, and introduce yourself to His Royal Cuteness.

b. Muster the guts to ask one of the people you know to introduce you to him.

c. Avoid eye contact—he probably has a girlfriend. Plus, you don't want him to dis you in front of your classmates.

7. Your parents leave town and give you strict "no party" instructions. At 9 p.m., a group of your pals ring the doorbell, ready to rumba. You . . .

a. Fling your door open wide and shout, "Let the party begin!"

b. Grab your coat and meet them outside. Maybe you can't host a party, but no parents means no curfew!

c. Hide in the dark and later lie through your braces. "Doorbell? What doorbell? I must have been drying my hair."

Scoring

Give yourself 3 points for every a, 2 points for every b, and 1 point for every c.

17 to 21 points: Daredevil Diva

You've never met a risk you didn't take, and your spontaneity makes you the life of the party. Once in a while, though, you leap (dive! bungee jump!) before you look and get into trouble.

A little prep work can help: Take a lesson before you ski Mt. Humongo, and make sure the girl with Mr. Perfect isn't his girlfriend before you slip him your number. You'll still have a thrillsville life—just without the occasional blush-producing blooper (or bone-breaking accident).

12 to 16 points: Reasonable Risker

With your great sense of adventure, you have the guts to try just about anything—within reason. But you also know when it's time to be careful, like when you strap on a helmet before climbing onto the back of your friend's motorbike. Feed your courage by reveling in past successes.

7 to 11 points: Safe Sister

Sometimes your "that-could-be-way-too-embarrassing" radar keeps you from doing things you might enjoy, like trying out for the soccer team. Start by taking little risks—accept an invite you'd normally nix or say hi to someone you don't know well. Soon, taking a chance will get much easier.

HOW TO TAKE THE PLUNGE

Making positive changes in your life means taking chances. Scared? Try these tips:

- Set your goal. Close your eyes and visualize what you want—and how great it will feel when you get it.

- Start small. Break goals into steps and tackle one step at a time.

- Get inspired. Talk to or read about someone who's accomplished a similar goal and learn from her experiences.

- Expect mistakes. Just figure out what went wrong and think about what you could do differently next time.

WHAT KIND OF FRIEND ARE YOU?

This, CosmoGIRL!, is why you are loved so much!

1. When your best friend gets dumped, you:

a. Spend hours listening to her. *(circled)*
b. Help her craft a letter telling the loser why she's glad he's gone.
c. Take her out for ice cream.
d. Share your dating disasters.

2. Your best friend has a big date. She's nervous so you:

a. Help her get ready.
b. Tell her he's lucky to be with her.
c. Go shopping with her in search of an awesome dress. *(circled)*
d. Lend her your sexiest jeans.

3. You hear a scandalous secret about someone. You:

a. Tell the person everyone's talking about her. *(circled)*
b. Take it to your grave.
c. Tell everyone to stop blabbing.
d. Let everyone pry it out of you.

4. Which of the following colors best reflects your true personality? Is it:

a. Purple—calm and collected.
b. Red—strong and determined. *(circled)*
c. Orange—dynamic and fun.
d. Blue—soothing and easy-going.

5. When your friends are hanging out, you:

a. Play the role of Dear Abby.
b. Laugh hard at everyone's jokes—even if they're bombs.
c. Suggest taking a road trip. *(circled)*
d. Pick up the tab.

6. Who is your favorite character on the television show *Friends*?

a. Rachel.
b. Either Phoebe or Joey.
c. Monica. *(circled)*
d. Either Ross or Chandler.

157

Scoring

Did you end up with a tie? Your type totally depends on who your friend is. So read 'em both!

mostly a's: The Confidante

You're the person your friends trust the most. They know they can turn to you when they need to vent—no matter what time of day (or night!) it may be. You really, *really* listen—and of course, give thoughtful advice

mostly b's: 100 Percent Devoted

You're the one who can always be counted on. No matter what happens, you stand behind your friends through thick and thin. It's your true-blue devotion that makes you so popular—when you make a friend, you're that persons friend for life.

mostly c's: The Motivator

You're always there to pick up the pieces when things go wrong, or to cheer your friends on when things go *right.* You draw out people's best qualities, which makes them want to follow your lead.

mostly d's: The Giver

You're a "what's mine is yours" kind of girl—you go out of your way to share everything from clothes to advice. That selfless attitude is wonderful, but don't let people take advantage of your generosity!

HOW FAR WOULD YOU GO FOR YOUR FRIENDS?

Would you walk on hot coals—or just little pebbles—to be by her side?

1. Your friend has a huge crush. You:

a. Throw a party and invite him—so they can finally hang out.
b. Flatter her when he's within earshot.
c. Help her map out a flirting strategy.

2. When she misses a week of classes before a test, you:

a. Pull an all-nighter to help her cram.
b. Photocopy your notes for her.
c. Buy her a cutesy good-luck pencil.

3. Your crush asks you out, but you already have plans with a friend. You:

a. Ask him for a rain check.
b. See your friend—then meet him later.
c. Reschedule her.

4. You're both interviewing for the same job. You:

a. Withdraw your application.
b. Go for the job and encourage her to too.
c. Say, "May the best woman win!"

5. She can't afford to go on spring break. You:

a. Skip it—and have fun at home together.
b. Lend her $200 in baby-sitting money.
c. Bring her back kitschy souvenirs.

6. She dropped her bracelet in the toilet at school. You:

a. Reach in to get it.
b. Help her find a random contraption to use to fish it out.
c. Crack up with her as she reaches in!

159

You'd go . . .

mostly a's: **Above and beyond**

Your unwavering loyalty is impressive! But make sure you go out of your way for friends because you truly want to—not because you think you *have* to. True friends will understand that you need to put *yourself* first sometimes. Because being a good friend doesn't mean meeting their needs at all costs— it means being there for someone who's there for you too.

mostly b's: **All the way**

You love your friends, and you're there to help them as much as you can. You have a finely tuned sense of when it's appropriate to drop what you're doing for someone else and when you need to focus on your own needs. You see friend- ship as a two-way street, and the people who are closest to you return the energy you put out for them by being there for you. Put simply, you've learned the fine art of *mutual* respect.

mostly c's: **A step or two**

You enjoy being with your friends—and you'll be there for them as long as doing so doesn't interfere with your own priorities or plans. It's good that you don't let yourself get off track, but every once in a while, going out of your way when a friend needs you is just the right thing to do. You know that whole saying about a friend in need being a friend indeed? Well, it's true!

for
fun

ANALYZE THIS!

Grab a pen and see what your handwriting reveals about you.

People don't have to read your journal to discover your inner secrets—they can find out just by looking at your history notes! "Huh?" you say? Well, it has to do with your script: Your strokes, slants, and structure hint at different aspects of your character. Experts believe emotional signals connect with those mechanical commands that shoot from the brain to control the movements guiding your pen. So write the sentence below in script to find out what you're revealing.

You and your silly monkey do not go home to the zoo on Friday.

You and your silly monkey do not go to the zoo on Friday.

Look at your *t*. Is it . . .

To	*to*
Crossed up high	**Crossed low**
You're full of confidence and ambition, so you continually set the bar higher for yourself. That strong sense of self will lead you to success and happiness.	You evaluate yourself every chance you get. This helps you catch your mistakes before others even notice them—but be sure you don't focus only on your flaws.

Look at your *m*. Does it have . . .

monkey

Round humps

You're at the top of your game when you take time to learn the facts you need to know. And once you've got that info down, it'll stay with you practically forever!

monkey

Jagged humps

You have a lightning-fast mind, which helps when cramming for exams or memorizing people's names. But take time to review the stuff you want to know long term.

Look at your *o*. Is it . . .

zoo

Looped to the right

You're a private person who's great at keeping secrets. Since opening up is hard for you, if you want to get stuff off your chest, try writing a letter to a friend.

zoo

Looped to the left

You're good at hiding your anxiety from others. But an issue can really gnaw at you sometimes, so jot down whatever comes to mind until you identify what's bugging you.

zoo

Double-looped

You tend to tell white lies to spare others' feelings. But you may cause more harm than good: People might not trust you when they find out you tell tales.

zoo

Open, no loops

You give your honest opinion—whether anyone asks or not. But that can be hurtful, so speak up when necessary, but be sure to think about what you're saying first.

Look at your *y*. Does it have a . . .

Big lower loop

You take what people say at face value, which is great. But others aren't always right—so ask questions to learn the facts. In the process, you'll gain more knowledge.

Right upstroke

You tend to let tension build up. Unload some of your stress by doing something physical— try heading out for a jog or shooting some hoops to really unwind.

Slight or no loop

Your fear of getting hurt makes it hard for you to trust. Let down your guard by sharing small things with those you're close to and slowly working up to the big stuff.

Look at your *slant*. Does it go . . .

To the right

You feel everything deeply—whether it's happiness or sadness. Be sure you don't let emotions get the best of you— share your thoughts with an even-keeled friend.

To the left

You care deeply about others, but you can come across as aloof because you're not that demonstrative. So be sure to tell people what you're feeling more often.

Upward

You have a great, balanced approach to life and decision making. Your ability to see the bright side of things helps you rise above any obstacles you face.

Want write-on improvements?

Build the character traits you want by adjusting your handwriting. Like, if you cross your *t*'s higher, you'll *feel* more confident in 30 days. Try it!

GET INTO YOUR ELEMENT!

Chinese philosophers believed every personality could be linked with one of five natural elements. Take this quiz to find yours!

1. If you joined the drama club at your school, you'd most likely be:

a. The director, leading the way.
b. The star of the show, of course!
c. The stage manager, taking care of all the actors' needs.
d. On the design crew, making sets and figuring out how to set them up.
e. The visionary playwright.

2. When you're channel surfing, which show always makes you stop and put down the remote control and watch it?

a. *The Apprentice.*
b. *The E! True Hollywood Story.*
c. A movie on Lifetime.
d. *CSI.*
e. *Smallville.*

3. If your best friends had to describe you with only one word, which of the following do you think they'd probably choose?

a. Competitive.
b. Dramatic.
c. Nurturing.
d. Organized.
e. Introspective.

4. You'd feel the most relaxed and be the happiest in which one of these environments?

a. A redwood forest, surrounded by the biggest and tallest of trees.
b. The hot, sun-soaked tropics.
c. A flower-filled meadow.
d. On top of a snow-covered mountain.
e. Near an ocean or a lake.

5. You find a hundred-dollar bill on the street. You:

a. Invest it so you'll make more.
b. Spend it all immediately.
c. Give it to a homeless person.
d. Figure out how to track down its owner—ASAP.
e. Wonder why you found it and what you were destined to do with it.

6. It's winter break! Which class's extra-credit assignment would you actually enjoy working on during your vacation?

a. Business.
b. Public speaking.
c. Art.
d. Math.
e. Philosophy.

Scoring

Which letter did you circle most often?
Match up that letter with your element below!

mostly a's: Wood

color: green

symbol: dragon

planet: Jupiter

your personality: You always aim high, looking to grow and expand—just like a tree. But at the same time your feet are firmly rooted and you approach your goals in a patient, rational way. Plus, your competitive and assertive nature and your quick problem-solving skills make you an excellent leader. It's hard for you to convey deep emotions, but it's easy for you to express yourself in a power position.

power tip: Keep a small tree like a bonsai in your room to help enhance your inner wood energy.

mostly b's: Fire

color: red

symbol: phoenix

planet: Mars

your personality: Like a fire, you're bright, intriguing, and quick to grab people's attention. You approach everything you do with passion and enthusiasm and are always up for trying new and adventurous things. You thrive on variety, so you can sometimes get frustrated or impatient when things become routine. Your friends love being around you because of your courage, charisma, and sociable energy!

power tip: Put a red night-light in your room to strengthen that fiery energy of yours.

mostly c's: Earth

color: yellow

symbol: cauldron

planet: Saturn

your personality: Like the earth's soil, you're very nurturing. You make a trustworthy, reliable friend and always have a shoulder ready for anyone to cry on. When problems come your way, you tend to work them out in a fair, practical manner. Although you worry a lot about things you can't control, you feel safe and calm when surrounded by family or close friends. You're low-key, you don't get worked up easily, and overall, you're very . . . well, down-to-earth!

power tip: Grow a flowering plant in a terra-cotta pot in your room to nurture your inner earth energy.

mostly d's: Metal

color: white

symbol: tiger

planet: Venus

your personality: You're persistent, and once you make up your mind, you're hard to bend—like metal itself! Very organized and disciplined, you'll see a task through to the end, no matter how long it takes. You have inner and outer strength and enjoy physical challenges. You see life as a puzzle to be solved logically, and you love to analyze new ideas and people. Use your self-control to keep that negativity you sometimes give off in check.

power tip: Display a small dish of coins in your room to help activate your inner metal energy.

mostly e's: Water

color: blue

symbol: tortoise

planet: Mercury

your personality: You're deep and mysterious, like the ocean. As an emotional, sensitive, and spiritual soul, you're constantly in search of honesty and truth in life. You enjoy spending introspective time alone to think and dream. You also have keen intuition, which makes you a great listener. But you'd much rather daydream than deal with some of life's harsher realities, like facing conflict.

power tip: If you set up a small aquarium with fish in your room, it will help reinforce your inner water energy.

WHAT'S YOUR CUP O' JOE?

See exactly where your personality falls on the beverage menu!

1. At parties, you usually:
a. Talk to the shy girl.
b. Wish you'd stayed in with your friends.
c. Chill out in a side room with the coolest people there.
d. Invent games!

2. What's your most prized possession?
a. Photos of your family and friends.
b. Your journal.
c. Your poetry.
d. Your goofy pet rock collection.

3. The one TV show you make sure never to miss is:
a. *Ugly Betty.*
b. *Buffy the Vampire Slayer* repeats.
c. *Smallville.*
d. *One Tree Hill.*

4. Where did you buy your favorite coat this year?
a. At a cute local boutique.
b. In a high-tech sporting goods store.
c. At an antique fair.
d. On eBay.

5. Which major appeals to you?
a. Social work or medicine.
b. Law, business, or communications.
c. Art or philosophy.
d. I'll create my own major.

6. What would you be most likely to get detention for?
a. Talking in class.
b. Cutting class.
c. Refusing to play hockey in gym.
d. Leading a sit-in to protest school policy.

You're like a . . .

mostly a's: Vanilla Latte

You're full of natural sugar! You're a lovable, genuine, and positive presence. People turn to you when they need a sympathetic ear because of your sensitivity and knack for bringing comfort to tough situations.

mostly b's: Espresso Forte

You're robust. You're strong in flavor and don't need excessive froufrou in your life. You may seem too bitter for some people, but those who *really* know you appreciate your no-nonsense attitude—you get things done and tell it like it is.

mostly c's: Kenya AA

You're mysterious and exotic. Deeply spiritual, you seek out knowledge, understanding, and adventure—which makes you anything but ordinary! People rely on you to help them see things from a new perspective.

mostly d's: Iced Mint-O-Chino

You're eclectic. People describe you as quirky and full of surprises because your presence sparks things up in any room. Spending time with you is a totally refreshing way to amp up even the *most* mundane situations!

WHAT'S YOUR BEAUTY STYLE?

Whether you're catching waves, cuties, or rays (or all three), take our quiz and find out which summer beauty goodies are perfect for your personality.

1. Your favorite treat on a really hot summer day is:

a. Sorbet.
b. Mocha Frappuccino.
c. Fruit yogurt smoothie.

2. If you could score your dream car, you'd pick:

a. A sleek import with a sunroof.
b. A convertible.
c. An SUV.

3. The star you'd most like to trade lives with for a day is:

a. Natalie Portman.
b. Beyoncé Knowles.
c. Cameron Diaz.

4. Between bands at an outdoor summer music festival, you're most likely to be found:

a. Buying concert T-shirts for all of your friends.
b. Scoping out ways to sneak backstage to meet the band.
c. Playing a game of Frisbee with the hot guys on the next blanket.

5. You're so predictable— people laugh at the fact that you:

a. Always pack a cardigan in case you happen to get cold.
b. Take four hours to get ready, even if you're just going to the grocery store.
c. Love to win at everything— even silly card games like Go Fish!

6. The guy who's driving you wild right now is:

a. Prince William—gorgeous eyes, sexy accent . . . he's a real prince!

b. **Orlando Bloom**—rugged good looks and always dressed to kill!

c. LeBron James—rockin' bod, major talent, and a Nike contract!

7. On the weekend, you're most likely to be found:

a. Doing volunteer work.

b. **At the mall scooping up the latest hair stuff and makeup—and a few outfits too.**

c. Working out early when the gym's not so crowded.

8. If you could win a major shopping spree to any store, which one would you pick?

a. J. Crew—they have so many adorable bathing suits.

b. **Sephora**—they have the coolest new hair and makeup stuff.

c. Niketown—they have gear for everything from hiking to surfing.

9. At Blockbuster, the section you immediately run to is:

a. Romance—you love movies with sappy (but happy) endings.

b. **New releases**—who cares about all the old boring ones?!

c. Action—fast-paced movies loaded with cool stunts are the best way to get an adrenaline rush.

Scoring

Find your score below (isn't it scary how well we know you?).

mostly a's: Preppy

You always look put together, but you're not fussy about your makeup. You stick to soft, girlie colors that look natural and blend perfectly with your skin tone.

mostly b's: Glam

You have a knack for finding the hottest, newest stuff before anyone else. Plus, you choose cool things—and *always* know exactly which products celebs are using.

mostly c's: Sporty

You want a look that won't get in the way of your active lifestyle, so you pick makeup that won't give you the slip when you dive into the pool or get a little sweaty.

ARE YOU SUPERSTITIOUS?

Put down that Magic 8 Ball long enough to see if you rely too much on fate!

1. You're wearing a new shirt when your crush finally asks you out. You:

a. Don't wash it so it'll retain its power.
b. Wear it when you need a boost of luck.
c. Don't think twice.

2. A black cat prances directly in front of you. You:

a. Turn around and find a new route.
b. Gasp loudly, then laugh at yourself.
c. Make kissy-kissy noises at it.

3. A friend mentions that you're a shoo-in for class president. You:

a. Are sure she just jinxed the vote.
b. Cross your fingers and hope so.
c. Thank her.

4. Has the Ouija board ever freaked you out?

a. It's not that it freaks me out; I just value it so much that I only use it sparingly.
b. Once or twice.
c. Nah.

5. You don't talk about the future because you:

a. Think fate might play a joke on you.
b. Never know what might come up to change things.
c. Don't plan ahead.

6. Your compact shatters. You:

a. Brace yourself for years of bad luck.
b. Figure a small mirror can't do *that* much damage.
c. Are annoyed you need to replace it.

You're a . . .

mostly a's: Devout Follower

Your intuition tells you it's better to be safe than sorry. This superstitious side is a reflection of your faith in higher powers. But don't sell yourself short; your fortune also owes a lot to your talent, skills, and hard work. Fate isn't the only force that shapes your life—you shape it too!

mostly b's: Believer

You aren't immune to the mysterious allure of rituals. But you tend to tap into fate only for an extra boost of luck—not because you think it'll be the one thing that actually determines your future. You realize chance plays a role in life but know it's what you do and don't do that really matters.

mostly c's: Doubter

You scoff at superstition. No one's going to catch you avoiding sidewalk cracks! With your logical disposition, you think you're the master of your own destiny. And that's great, because you know how to rely on yourself. Just don't judge others who believe a little magic helps!

FRIEND FORTUNE TELLER

Use our version of this old childhood game to see what the future holds for your friendship!

How to play: Make a copy of this so you can play with a friend. Fill in options for each category below. (Write four good possibilities and one really out-there one!) Then start drawing a spiral in the box below. When your friend yells "stop," stop! Count the lines across the spiral, then, starting at the letter F on page 186, move that number of spaces (so if it's four, you'll land on E); cross off E, then, starting at N, keep moving four spaces through the category lines top to bottom. Go through college, career, reunion, city, crush, crazy things, and back to FRIEND, crossing off options until only one is left per group. And that, CosmoGIRL!, is how your true friendship "future" will be revealed!

How close you'll live to each other . . .

| Flight Away | Room together | In the same city | Extremely far away | Next state over | Down the block |

which college you'll attend

_____
_____
_____
_____
_____

which career you'll have

_____
_____
_____
_____
_____

where you'll have an annual reunion

_____
_____
_____
_____
_____

which city you'll live in

_____
_____
_____
_____
_____

celeb crush you'll meet and date

_____
_____
_____
_____
_____

craziest things you'll do together

_____
_____
_____
_____
_____

WHAT COLOR IS YOUR AURA?

Take this quiz and unlock the secret to your inner self!

Directions: Answer each question in all six groups below and write in **yes** or **no** on the line provided. Be honest and say what you believe you truly are, not how you'd like to be. When you finish, check the next page to discover your aura. Ready to get glowing?

1.
I'd rather take action than discuss plans. ✓

I can get angry fast, ~~but I get over it quickly too.~~ ✓

It's pretty hard for me to express my feelings. ✓

Life is about the physical, not the spiritual. ✗

I prefer concrete ideas to abstract ones. ✗

2.
I crave independence and hate being tied down. ✓

I'm often involved in a lot of projects at once. ✓

I truly believe I can help to improve the world. ✗

I love performing in front of an audience. ✓

I feel I was put here to be important or famous. ✗

3.
I'm very sensitive and aware of others' feelings. ✓

I'm emotional and I tend to cry easily. ✓

I hate dealing with conflict or confrontation. ✗

I feel guilty if I have to say no to someone. ✗

Friends depend on me for a shoulder to cry on. ✓

4. ⌄

I enjoy being in charge and delegating work. ✗

I tend to be a perfectionist about most things. ✗

I like things to be organized and well planned. ✓

I love doing competitive activities or sports. ✗

I want a powerful job that pays a lot of money. ✓

5. 3

I tend to get frustrated if I'm not having fun. ✓

I'm optimistic and almost always smiling. ✗

I have lots of energy and detest sitting still. ✓

I'm always told I have a great sense of humor. ✗

I love doing things on the spur of the moment. ✓

6. ⌄

I often try to push beyond my physical limits. ✗

I'm always the first to accept any kind of dare. ✗

I love heart-racing things like roller coasters. ✓

There are few things that I'm afraid of. ✗

I'm a risk-taker and I live for adventure. ✓

WHAT'S AN AURA?

It's a group of invisible bands of colored light that surround all living things. Each color has been found to relate to certain personality traits.

Scoring: Tally up your yeses from each group of questions. The group with the most yeses is your aura. Match that group number with its corresponding color on the following pages. Have a tie? You have a *combination* aura—your personality reflects more than one color. But whether you have just one aura or several of them, what's important is that it's the essence of *you*!

189

#1: Red

Personality
With your zest and self-confidence, you live in the here and now. You like to experience the world through taste, touch, and smell, and are happiest when working.

School
When confronted with a difficult problem, you face it with determination. You never let it go unsolved, no matter how long it takes to figure out.

Love
It can be hard for you to open up since you're a very private person. You need someone secure who won't misinterpret your independence.

Career
Your ideal job is one where you control the outcome and have something tangible to show for your work, like being a chef, surgeon, or carpenter.

#2: Violet

Personality
You're a visionary and a dreamer who feels you were put here to do something great. Your flair for the dramatic and your strong charisma will help you make a lasting impact on the world.

School
You love getting involved as a leader in many clubs and take on extra-credit assignments.

Love

You're passionate, but you get so busy inspiring others that you don't have much time for love. You need someone to recognize your vision and work beside you to achieve it.

Career

You'll get the most satisfaction by working for yourself in a job where you feel you make a difference, such as being a teacher, politician, or musician.

#3: Blue

Personality

As a born caretaker, your warmth and intuition help you nurture those around you. In life you follow your heart and believe that everyone should be accepted.

School

Since you're emotional, you stress out easily. But when you quietly sit and get centered, you're always able to regroup and do what needs to be done.

Love

Relationships are your top priority and you get unhappy when you're not in one. You're happiest spending a lot of time with one committed person.

Career

You work best in one-on-one situations and are drawn to fields where you take care of others, such as nursing, psychology, or counseling.

Personality

You're a high-achiever whose aim is to take on the world. You love being in control and hate to be wrong. Your quick thinking and competitive nature will help you meet any goal that you set for yourself.

School

Because you can't stand to fail, you'll push yourself incredibly hard to always be number one. You are a fast learner and love a good mental challenge.

Love

With such high standards, you may find it hard to meet your match. You need someone as goal-oriented and driven as you.

Career

You would thrive in the high-profile, lucrative role of a stockbroker, CEO, or salesperson, or by working solo as an entrepreneur.

#5: Yellow

Personality

You feel life's too short to take too seriously, so you seek out things that make you happy. You're fun-loving, energetic, and like to bring joy to those around you.

School

You'd rather be playing, but when you must work, you rely on creativity and humor to help develop unique ideas.

Love

You love to flirt, and since you need freedom, it scares you to be tied down. But once you do find that person who makes you feel safe, you're very loyal.

Career

Variety is key, so you'll probably have many jobs in your life, but all of them will let you have fun. Consider being an actress, writer, or comedian.

#6: Orange

Personality

Physical challenges don't faze you one bit, and you feel most alive when faced with adventure or danger. You're a thrill-seeking daredevil who prefers to be constantly on the go.

School

You attack each test or project with intensity, analyzing all the possible solutions and then jumping right into action.

Love

Only another adventurer will do—you can challenge each other and live life in the fast lane!

Career

You need a high-risk job with flexible hours so you can travel and find adventure too. Think forensic detective, stunt double, or police officer.

TIME TO FENG SHUI!

So what if you can't pronounce it.
This Chinese philosophy can make your room—
and your world—a happier place.

1. How is your bed positioned in your room?

a. The head of the bed is right under a window.
b. The headboard is against a wall, and you have a full view of the door—but are not directly across from it.
c. The headboard is along the same wall as the door.

2. Okay, be honest: How would you describe the clutter in your bedroom?

a. Almost nonexistent. You're a neat freak!
b. You try to clean regularly, but somehow it always seems to pile up again.
c. You haven't seen your floor in ages.

3. How many electronic items in your bedroom are plugged in?

a. Three or four, and they're scattered all around the room.
b. No more than two or three, and they're all at least 3 feet away from your bed.
c. Tons, and a bunch of them surround your bed.

4. When you're sitting at your desk:

a. You have your back to the door.
b. You have a blank wall less than 3 feet in front of you.
c. You have a clear view of the main doorway to your room.

5. Your bedroom walls are covered with:

a. Music, movie, and TV posters.
b. Shelves of dolls and/or things from your past.
c. A mix of photos of friends, family, and some celebs.

6. Your closet doors:

a. Open and close easily *and* don't have any mirrors or pictures.
b. Have mirrors hanging on the front of them.
c. Get stuck or jammed all the time in their tracks or on their hinges.

Answer Key

By following feng shui to move items to certain places, you can create a balanced environment that will influence all aspects of your life. Can't move things to their optimal positions? Try our quick fixes.

1. The Bed: Optimal answer is b

Why: If it faces your door, you'll be calmer and more serene, since no one will be able to sneak in or startle you. Chose *a* or *c*? Set up a mirror in the room so that you can see the reflection of your door from your bed.

2. The Clutter: Optimal answer is a

Why: Clean, organized areas sharpen your mental clarity. Chose *b* or *c*? If you really can't stay neat, hang a set of wind chimes over the most cluttered area in your room. In feng shui, chimes attract attention and help to focus you.

3. The Electronic Items: Optimal answer is b

Why: Electronically charged items sap your internal energy. Chose *a* or *c*? Move your gadgets as far from the bed as you can. Put them in a cabinet when they're not in use.

4. The Desk: Optimal answer is c

Why: A door view opens a path to leadership opportunities. Chose *a* or *b*? Prop a mirror on your desk to see the reflection of the door behind you, or hang a picture that has depth (like a landscape) on the wall in front of you.

5. The Walls: Optimal answer is c

Why: Images of familiar faces lead to better communication. Chose *a* or *b*? Can't part with your past or your posters? Find a happy medium: Pack up half of them and replace the rest with pictures of your friends and family.

6. The Closet: Optimal answer is a

Why: Clean, free-moving doors help you make progress. Chose *b* or *c*? Repair doors and cover mirrors with plain white fabric so you won't get stuck in a rut.

Find out if you're the cowgirl who knows how to get the party started! (Yee-haw!)

1. What are you doing for April Fools' Day?

a. Nothing. April Fools' Day is for kids.

b. Putting salt in the sugar bowl and sugar in the salt shaker.

c. Punking *all* day!

2. Your ideal birthday plans are:

a. A whole day of pampering yourself.

b. Having dinner with a bunch of really close friends.

c. A blowout party that goes on all night!

3. When the kids you baby-sit get way too hyper, you:

a. Get the oldest kid to help you calm them.

b. Play tag until they're exhausted.

c. Reverse roles and go kooky on *them.*

4. What's your top career priority?

a. Helping people so you can make a difference in the world.

b. Making big bucks.

c. Finding ways to make the most of your creativity.

5. When your last Friday class gets out early, you:

a. Get a head start on your homework.

b. Relax at home.

c. Round up the girls to hang at your place.

6. It's family reunion time. You:

a. Help your mom make potato salad.

b. Catch up with your favorite cousins.

c. Crack everyone up with your Grandma Sadie impersonation.

You're a . . .

mostly a's: Party Goer

You're mature and responsible—you don't have to go crazy to have fun, and you rarely give in to peer pressure to do something you don't really want to do. That attitude has earned you trust and respect. But remember: Letting your hair down every now and then is key to staying healthy—emotionally and physically—because it gives you a more well-rounded life. So when *your* inner child wants to come out and play, let her!

mostly b's: Party Girl

You like to have fun—without going overboard. You're a master at balancing work and play. And when you want to have a good time, you tend to stick to things that are tried and true. Still, there may be times when you'll get pulled to be more spontaneous and less serious—or to sacrifice fun in the name of hard work. When that happens, trust that your level-headed approach will steer you in the right direction.

mostly c's: Party Animal

Life's a big party to you—you *make* fun happen! You're silly and creative, and you pride yourself on keeping yourself—and your friends—entertained. But that carefree spirit might make some people think they can't take you seriously or rely on you. So make an effort to show that you can be fun and trust-worthy at the same time by following through on your responsibilities at home and school, and with friends.

HOW WELL DO YOU KNOW HER?

Everyone knows about her size-10 1/2 feet and her insane crush on Orlando, but some things you share only with your closest friend.

Directions: Starting with the right column, answer the first six questions about *yourself*, the next six (pg. 202, left) about your *friend*. Fold over your answers, then pass the book to her. On the left, she'll answer six questions about *you* and six (pg. 202, right) about *herself*. Compare. Is it like you're mind readers? Yay! If not, a few late-night gabfests over Ben & Jerry's will do it!

About Her		About Me
- - - - - - - - - - - - - - - - - -	1. Your/her most amazing accomplishment so far:	- - - - - - - - - - - - - - - - - -
- - - - - - - - - - - - - - - - - -		- - - - - - - - - - - - - - - - - -
- - - - - - - - - - - - - - - - - -	2. The first store at the mall you go/she goes to:	- - - - - - - - - - - - - - - - - -
- - - - - - - - - - - - - - - - - -		- - - - - - - - - - - - - - - - - -
- - - - - - - - - - - - - - - - - -	3. Name three items in your/her bag right now:	- - - - - - - - - - - - - - - - - -
- - - - - - - - - - - - - - - - - -		- - - - - - - - - - - - - - - - - -
- - - - - - - - - - - - - - - - - -	4. Have you/has she ever been in love? With who?	- - - - - - - - - - - - - - - - - -
- - - - - - - - - - - - - - - - - -		- - - - - - - - - - - - - - - - - -
- - - - - - - - - - - - - - - - - -	5. The last time you/she cried was because:	- - - - - - - - - - - - - - - - - -
- - - - - - - - - - - - - - - - - -		- - - - - - - - - - - - - - - - - -
- - - - - - - - - - - - - - - - - -	6. In 10 years, where do you see yourself/her?	- - - - - - - - - - - - - - - - - -
- - - - - - - - - - - - - - - - - -		- - - - - - - - - - - - - - - - - -

Fold in here to hide your answers and pass this quiz to a friend.

	About Her		About Me
- - - - - - - - - - - - - - - - - -	**1. Your/her most**		- - - - - - - - - - - - - - - - - -
	amazing accom-		
- - - - - - - - - - - - - - - - - -	**plishment so far:**		- - - - - - - - - - - - - - - - - -
- - - - - - - - - - - - - - - - - -	**2. The first store at**		- - - - - - - - - - - - - - - - - -
	the mall you go/she		
- - - - - - - - - - - - - - - - - -	**goes to:**		- - - - - - - - - - - - - - - - - -
- - - - - - - - - - - - - - - - - -	**3. Name three items**		- - - - - - - - - - - - - - - - - -
	in your/her bag right		
- - - - - - - - - - - - - - - - - -	**now:**		- - - - - - - - - - - - - - - - - -
- - - - - - - - - - - - - - - - - -	**4. Have you/has she**		- - - - - - - - - - - - - - - - - -
	ever been in love?		
- - - - - - - - - - - - - - - - - -	**With who?**		- - - - - - - - - - - - - - - - - -
- - - - - - - - - - - - - - - - - -	**5. The last time**		- - - - - - - - - - - - - - - - - -
	you/she cried was		
- - - - - - - - - - - - - - - - - -	**because:**		- - - - - - - - - - - - - - - - - -
- - - - - - - - - - - - - - - - - -	**6. In 10 years, where**		- - - - - - - - - - - - - - - - - -
	do you see your-		
- - - - - - - - - - - - - - - - - -	**self/her?**		- - - - - - - - - - - - - - - - - -

Fold in here to hide your answers and pass this quiz to a friend.

Discover Your Secret Self

You & Your Friends

You & Guys

ARE YOU CATTY?

Find out if you're too quick to whip out your claws—or if you act more like the runt of the litter.

1. When you see a girl you know wearing the same shirt you wanted to buy, you tell her:

a. "I tried that on but I thought it looked cheap, so I put it back."

b. "I love your shirt!"—and find one like it (but better) that weekend.

c. "I was thinking of getting that, but it looks better on you, so I'm not even going to try it on now."

2. Your best friend's boyfriend has been flirting with you like crazy lately. What do you do?

a. Flirt back and then bad-mouth him to your friend.

b. Be nice to him but don't encourage or flirt back.

c. Avoid him at all costs and hope your friend doesn't find out.

3. You're hanging out with a group of people and notice that a girl you don't like has spinach in her teeth. Your next move?

a. Call it out in front of everyone, knowing it will embarrass her.

b. Keep quiet—hey, she wouldn't tell you if you had green teeth.

c. Pretend you don't see it.

4. A cute girl drops her bag and your boyfriend runs to help her pick up her stuff. You:

a. Ask her if she has her period when you see a tampon roll out.

b. Go and help them, of course.

c. Walk away; if he wants to flirt with her, there's nothing you can do about it.

5. You're playing volleyball in P.E. and your boyfriend's ex is on the other team. You make it a point to:

a. "Accidentally" nail her with a spike—right between the eyes.
b. Try your hardest not to focus on her.
c. Tell the teacher you're sick so you can sit out the game.

6. You and a friend are getting ready for a party and she asks your opinion about a not-so-flattering outfit she's trying on. You say:

a. "Totally wear it—it looks fabulous!"
b. "I'm not feeling it . . . what about the jeans you had on before?"
c. "You look great in everything, but that's not my favorite one."

7. You hear that a girl you know is spreading rumors about your best friend. What do you do?

a. Start spreading rumors about her. She deserves it, the little witch!
b. Find out if she really said that stuff and give your friend the full report.
c. Stay out of it—you'll just make the situation worse than it already is.

8. You're going to a party this weekend. Your crush will be there—along with another girl who likes him. When you get there, you:

a. Get them both together, then ask the girl something like, "Remember when you farted in math class on Monday? That was hilarious!"
b. Get him alone and banter with him to see whether he likes you back.
c. Let her have him—she probably has a better chance anyway.

Scoring

mostly a's: Hiss!

You may not realize you're being catty but it seems like you often put other girls down to build yourself up. Even if you've been wronged in the past, remind yourself that other girls aren't always the enemy. Try to put more purr in your personality—it pays off way more than playing dirty!

mostly b's: Meow!

You've got a healthy attitude toward other girls and don't see them as rivals. You know there's enough happiness to go around—so you don't sweat it if someone else is on top for a bit. Your claws do come out now and then, but it's usually when you have to defend yourself. Good kitty!

mostly c's: Mew!

You're like a defenseless kitten, vulnerable to the whims of others—friends or enemies. Maybe you hold back because you're shy, but you need to fight harder for the respect you deserve. Next time, don't curl up in a ball to give others the right of way—speak up and let your thoughts be heard. Rowr!

ARE YOU A GOSSIP JUNKIE?

If gossip were a drug it'd be an out-of-control substance. Come clean and find out if you might need some rehab.

1. The best reason to have a profile on MySpace is to:

a. Keep tabs on your ex.
b. Check out photos on other people's profiles.
c. Listen to songs of new indie bands.

2. Huge news! You just found out one of the popular girls at school got liposuction. How long do you keep it to yourself?

a. Keep it? You're mass-texting people now!
b. Until someone else blabs, then you're ready to dish!
c. Forever. You don't know her so it's not your business.

3. When it comes to celebrity gossip, you:

a. Live for it— perezhilton.com is your home page!
b. Think it's entertaining— you'll flip through *US Weekly* at the nail salon.
c. They write gossip about celebs?

4. You're arriving home from spending a semester in Italy. You call your friends:

a. You texted them every day anyway!
b. After you've caught up with your family.
c. After you've unpacked and taken a long nap to fight jet lag.

5. You see the book "Why Men Have Affairs" on your friend Julie's living room table. You:

a. Tell your friends the second you leave her house!
b. Wait until you're alone and then ask Julie what's up.
c. Ignore it.

Scoring

mostly a's: Bad habit

Being loaded with the latest gossip can feel empowering, but broadcasting it to the world can lead to trouble. If you keep sharing people's secrets they'll stop trusting you. Be wise: Those who talk get talked about . . . and even you probably have some skeletons you want to keep in the closet!

mostly b's: Mildly addicted

A little healthy dishing makes you feel connected. But while you appreciate the rush of hearing a juicy rumor, you also know when to resist the urge to spread it around. And that's good news since the gossip chain is only fun until someone—maybe even you—gets hurt.

mostly c's: Squeaky clean

When it comes to gossip, you've got "earmuffs" on 24/7! But by not turning into the rumor mill, you may be missing out on what's happening around you—both good and bad. So unplug those ears and give it a whirl—it's okay to indulge every so often.

CAN YOUR FRIENDS COUNT ON YOU?

When the poo hits the fan, do you run for cover or stick around to help clean up the mess?

1. Your closest friends are most likely to call you when they need someone to help them:

a. With their guy problems.
b. Cover up the dent they put in their dad's car.
c. Throw a party.

2. Two of your friends get in a huge fight, so when one calls you to talk about it, you automatically:

a. Get the other on three-way and help them work it out.
b. Listen to her vent, but don't take sides.
c. Say, "Oh, don't worry, it'll blow over."

3. Your friend asks you to read her college application but you just don't feel like it. You:

a. Do it anyway and give her suggestions that night.
b. Do it but take a half an hour to go over it.
c. Lie and tell her you don't have time.

4. At a party, you're talking to a hot guy when you notice that your friend is stuck with a major loser. You:

a. Run right over and help her escape.
b. Rescue her if she rolls her eyes at you.
c. Keep chatting up Señor Sweetie.

5. Your friend gets bad news: Her 70-year-old aunt has died, and she's really upset. What do you do?

a. Bring over cookies you baked for her family.
b. Give her a sympathy card.
c. Leave her alone—she probably wants her space.

6. You find out that your best friend's crush actually has a thing for a girl you both hate. When do you tell your friend?

a. Right away. It's better she hears it from you.
b. You wait until she's not stressed.
c. Never! You hate giving bad news.

Scoring

mostly a's: No doubt about it!

You'd do anything for your girls and they know it! But if you're constantly all over their lives, they might feel crowded—especially those times they're not looking for help. So think before you act and ask yourself, does she need advice, or does she just need a shoulder to cry on? Your friends will love you even more!

mostly b's: That depends

Your friends line up to see you for advice. You don't like to ask your friends for help, but they know you need support once in a while (everyone does!) So ask them for help when little stress-balls hit. They'll be flattered you did and eager to return the favor.

mostly c's: Don't count on it

Everyone loves your good-time-girl attitude, but since you're so busy having fun, it can be hard for your friends to rely on you. Next time you sense a friend is worried or bummed out, ask, "What's wrong?" Let her know you're there and use that wicked sense of humor of yours to help cheer her up. When you share the good times and the bad, you both win.

WHO CONTROLS YOUR LIFE?

Find out if your friends' opinions really matter or if you march to the beat of a different drum.

1. You're at a party and your favorite song comes on. No one is dancing, so you:

a. Stay put and start tapping your foot.
b. Grab your friend and make her dance with you.
c. Get up anyway and show off your latest dance moves.

2. Your curfew is an hour earlier than everyone else's. On the night of the biggest party of the school year, you:

a. Try to have as much fun as possible before going home.
b. Tell your parents it's unfair and beg them to extend it by thirty minutes.
c. Stay out the extra hour anyway and risk the consequences.

3. Your friends are obsessed with a flick you hated. When the conversation turns to the movie you say:

a. "I loved it too!"
b. "It was okay—but I've seen better."
c. "It sucked. I want those hours back!"

4. You're totally into that adorable guy in your math class, but your friends all think he's a loser. You:

a. Reconsider your crush.
b. Give it a few days to decide on your own whether he has potential.
c. Think, "To each her own."

5. You might audition for the school play, but your friends don't think it's cool and try to talk you out of it. You:

a. Decide to stick to activities your friends do.

b. Persuade at least one of them to try out with you.

c. Nail your audition monologue and take the stage without them.

Scoring

mostly a's: Eager to Please

It's hard for you to make a move without running it past your friends. Of course you should value their opinions, but when you ignore your gut, you might be missing out on new, exciting opportunities. So don't be afraid to stand up for what you believe in—friends worth keeping will admire you all the more.

mostly b's: Thorough Thinker

You respect your friends' opinions—but you won't follow advice that you don't agree with. Keep on thinking things through and making the decisions that are right for you. Your friends will admire your strength and you might even inspire a few of them to branch out on their own once in a while.

mostly c's: Ms. Independent

You're full of self-confidence and you're not afraid to voice your opinion or try things that others might not. Stick to your guns, girl! If we all followed the crowd all the time, life would be boring. But your fierce daredevil streak leads you to amazing adventures that others might let pass them by—like the lead role in the school play!

ARE YOU A GOOD LISTENER?

Do you take it all in or let it all out? Find out if you're all ears, all mouth, or a bit of both!

1. You and your best friend just got back from being on (separate) vacations. How does the conversation go?

a. You tell every last detail of your trip.
b. You take turns telling all your fun stories.
c. She talks non-stop and you get filled in.

2. You friend calls you crying (*again!*) because her ex is dating a new girl. You're so sick of hearing about him! You:

a. Start talking about your ex to try and distract her.
b. Listen once more, but tell her she needs to move on.
c. Let her ramble on and are attentive as usual.

3. You're right in the middle of your favorite TV show when your friend calls to complain about school. What do you do?

a. Keep watching and just "uh huh" her every now and then.
b. Put the show on mute while she talks.
c. TiVo your show and give her your full attention.

4. You mom calls you with a list of things she needs you to do before you come home. You:

a. Are checking Facebook as she talks.
b. Hear the two most important tasks.
c. Write them all down as she tells you.

5. Your best friend just introduced you to her three bunk-mates from camp. Their names are:

a. Um, can I get name tags, please!

b. Jane, Sara, and you—forget the third.

c. Already stored in your brain, along with their hometowns, birthdays, and favorite bands!

Scoring

mostly a's: All mouth

You'd rather talk about yourself than listen to anyone else's problems. But acting like that shows people you don't care about your friendship, even if you do. And would you want to feel like your friends don't want to listen to your problems? No! So zip your lip every so often and give others the floor.

mostly b's: Half an ear

You try to concentrate on what your friends are saying, but sometimes you find yourself making a mental to-do list or day-dreaming of your latest celeb crush. Since you truly do care, try to make their conversation a priority. Turn off your cell and the TV and just listen for five minutes. You'll be glad you did— and so will they!

mostly c's: All ears

Now hear this—you're the best listener out there! When one of your friends needs to talk, she knows she can go to you and you'll be there to soak up every last word. But don't forget: Sometimes you need someone to listen to you too. Next time you're looking for advice, you can bet your friends will be more than happy to lend their ears.

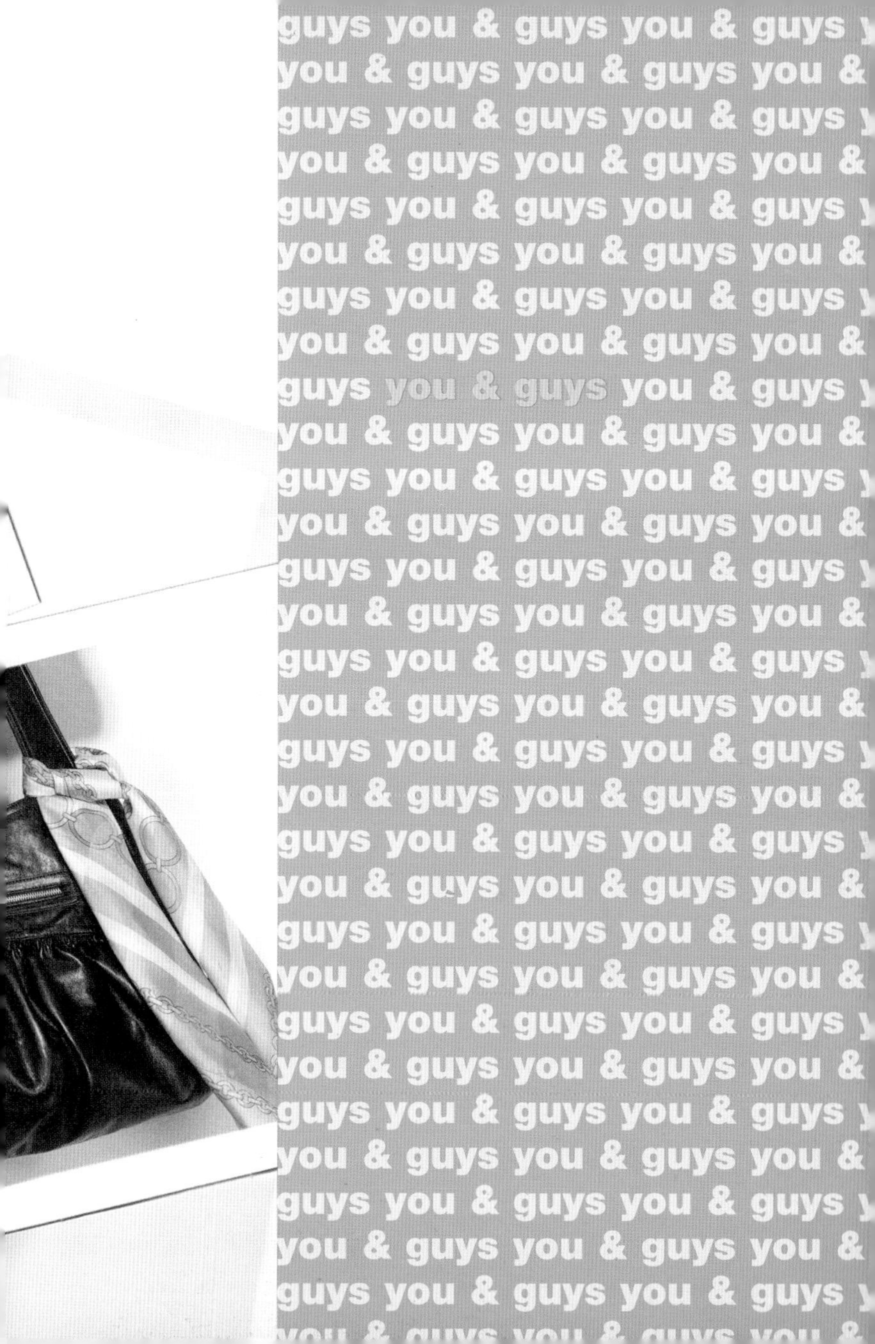
you & guys

ARE YOU A TEASE?

*Find out if you're the kind of girl
who (mercilessly!) misleads guys.*

**1. When you talk to a guy—
whether he's just a friend
or your crush—you tend to:**

a. Look down or away.
b. Make eye contact.
c. Giggle a lot and make
   physical contact, like
   touching his arm.

**2. When you try on outfits
for big events like prom,
who are you *really* hoping
you'll wow?**

a. Yourself.
b. Your friends.
c. Guys.

**3. When your best
friend's crush offers you
and her a ride home after
school, you:**

a. Sit like a church mouse in
   the backseat so they can
   have some time alone.
b. Mention one of your best
   friend's accomplishments
   from the backseat so she
   looks like a superstar in
   front of him.
c. Blurt out "Shotgun!" and
   chat him up.

**4. When a friend confides
in you that she's totally into
a certain guy, you:**

a. Let her talk about him
   nonstop.
b. Help her come up with
   strategies for getting him
   to pay attention to her.
c. Start flirting with him,
   secretly hoping he'll think
   you're cool.

**5. Do you ever bail on your
friends for a guy—even one
you may not be that into?**

a. No way, that's not your
   style—guys are not *that*
   much of a priority.
b. It's happened once or
   twice, at a party or something.
c. Yup: your friends joke that
   they have to drag you
   away from guys.

6. You find out that one of your guy friends would die to date you. You don't like him like that, so:

a. You stop calling him.
b. You make sure not to hang out alone with him, and you talk about your crushes in front of him.
c. You bring him to parties and everywhere else you go, and end up grinding with him on the dance floor in front of all your friends.

7. When a guy you meet from another school asks if he can call you, you say yes, because:

a. It would be awkward to say no, and you don't want to hurt his feelings.
b. You sincerely mean it: You'd want to see him again to find out more about him.
c. You just like being thought of as the girl who guys want—even if you have no intention of dating him.

8. Would you make out with a guy who was interested in you, even if you weren't interested in him?

a. No, that's gross.
b. Maybe—he might be a good kisser!
c. You'd go for a walk but not make out.

Scoring

The letter you picked most says if you're using that back comb way too much!

mostly a's: Polished Pixie

You're so shy when it comes to guys that you don't even really flirt! Guys may interpret your shyness as indifference, so try to overcome your fears in small ways: Make eye contact with your crush next time, okay CG!?

mostly b's: Va-va Vixen

You know how to engage a guy you like in a way that makes him feel good. You also know when to hold back— you wouldn't play with a guy's mind or lead on someone who simply doesn't stand a chance with you.

mostly c's: Teased-out Temptress

Trying to attract every guy you meet might give you a self-esteem charge, but it could hurt a guy's feelings—and earn you a bad rep. So seek out other confidence-boosters (like hobbies) and be more selective about who you flirt with.

ARE YOU DESPERATE?

Find out if you're way too obsessed with getting a boyfriend!

1. "Big News" for you means:

a. There's been a development with a guy.
b. Your parents are making your curfew later.
c. You aced a test you were nervous about.

2. You refuse to graduate without:

a. Dating a school sports captain.
b. Cheering on your school's M.V.P. at all of his important games.
c. Breaking a school sports record.

3. How many of your friends have boyfriends?

a. All of them.
b. Some of them.
c. None of them.

4. Would you ever turn down a guy who asked you out?

a. No. I'd rather have a lame date than no date.
b. Maybe. It depends on who it was.
c. If I wasn't interested I'd let him down easy.

5. Your best friend has a hot older cousin. You:

a. Constantly bug her to set you up with him.
b. Love when she brings him up so you can talk about him.
c. Strike up a conversation with him at her birthday party.

6. Ever act wild around guys at parties?

a. Yes.

b. That depends what your definition of wild is.

c. No.

7. When an "unknown caller" shows up on your cell, you:

a. Always pick up—it could be that guy!

b. Stress, but then usually pick it up at the last minute.

c. Let it go to voicemail.

8. Would you cancel plans with a friend for a last-minute date?

a. Most likely yes.

b. Well, only if he was really cute!

c. Probably not—unless I got her blessing first.

9. You tried out for the school play because:

a. The hottest senior in school was trying out.

b. You thought it would be a fun way to meet people.

c. You love acting.

Scoring*

mostly a's: **Very desperate**

Trying too hard drives guys away, girl! So throw yourself into *hobbies* you're passionate about and you'll be too busy to worry about having a boyfriend.

mostly b's: **Mildly desperate**

It's normal to feel lonely sometimes, but don't let the quest for a guy consume you. Instead, when you feel those "I don't have a boyfriend" blues coming on, have fun with friends who make you feel special!

mostly c's: **Me? Desperate?**

Because you're not dying for guys' attention, your confidence and independence actually end up *attracting* guys to you—all the time. Ironic, no?

*Your type doesn't quite sound like you? Sometimes we choose what we want to be, rather than what we are. So take the quiz again with a friend who can help you pick the most true-to-you answers!

WHAT KIND OF SEXY ARE YOU?

You have a certain something that just draws people to you! Find out what it is—and how you can use it to get the guy you want.

1. He's the first guy you've met in a while who can really make your heart jump. To let him know you're interested, you:

a. Smile and compliment his shirt.

b. Ask him what music's on his iPod.

c. Let him in on the secret move you discovered on *Halo 2.*

2. You and the guy you're into are in the same volunteer group. You love that you get to bond with him while:

a. Visiting lonely elderly people in your town.

b. Tutoring kids in math.

c. Blocking him in a super-sweaty charity basketball game.

3. You're going to a concert tonight and your crush will be there. You wouldn't leave home without:

a. A spritz of your favorite perfume—the scent just makes you feel irresistible!

b. A quirky conversation piece, like that manga book you've been reading.

c. A pair of earplugs—you'll want to get right up next to the stage for maximum noiseage.

4. Which actress would you cast to play you in a movie based on your life?

a. Jennifer Garner—you like the way she's always nice to everyone.

b. Natalie Portman—she seems to know just the right thing to say no matter what situation she's in.

c. Cameron Diaz—she's down-to-earth and not afraid to laugh at herself.

5. The cute guy in study hall has been giving you the eye almost every day. What do you do?

a. Hold his gaze a bit longer than normal, then look away coyly.

b. Write him a note that says, "Less looking, more talking. Let's get coffee!"

c. Challenge him to a staring contest—two can play at this game!

6. You're at a club when that Alicia Keys and Usher song "My Boo," starts playing. You:

a. Grab your crush and say, "Why of course you can have this dance!"

b. Ask him, "How would you like to sit out this song with me?"

c. Start fast-dancing to make him laugh, then ask him to do the robot.

7. You're talking to a cute guy at a party when he tells a "funny" story that seriously bombs. You:

a. Laugh anyway—you don't want him to be embarrassed!

b. Shake your head, smile, and say, "And it started out so promisingly!"

c. Change the subject by asking him to thumb-wrestle with you.

Scoring

Tally up your a's, b's, and c's.
Then see what makes you so darn sexy!

mostly a's: You're flirty

Guys are drawn to your sweet, girly charisma and rarely feel nervous around you. But don't feel you have to hide your true feelings just to spare theirs. Guys respect a girl who's not afraid to be honest.

mostly b's: You're sharp

You radiate smart-girl charm. Guys see you as a challenge, and it makes them feel great if a girl with such high standards gives them the time of day. But let your goofy side out too— you can be the girl who's brainy *and* fun!

mostly c's: You're fun

Your no-frills nature makes you a girl and a friend rolled into one—and guys think that rocks. But show the one you like your deeper, serious side too, so he sees you as a friend who could potentially be a girlfriend.

DO YOU SCARE GUYS AWAY?

No one can read a guy's mind, but here's your chance to find out if your crush thinks you're playing it cool—or a little crazy.

1. When you start liking a guy, your philosophy is:

a. He either likes you or not— so you might as well find out now instead of wasting time wondering.

b. He'd probably like you if he got to know you—why not make a move and see?

c. There's almost no chance he'd like you because he's way out of your league, but how perfect would it be if he did?

2. At kindergarten recess, you could usually be found:

a. Chasing a boy to kiss— a new one every week.

b. Playing in the sandbox with your friends—both boys and girls.

c. Forming a girls-only club to avoid those icky boys.

3. You run into your crush and all his friends at the mall. You:

a. Yell out his name, give him a big hug and talk only to him.

b. Stop and chat with his group of friends for a few minutes, but give him a compliment so you can single him out.

c. Talk to his friends—you just can't get up the nerve to talk to him (and you'd probably say something dumb anyway).

4. You've been talking to a cute guy at school, but neither of you has made a move. Your next step:

a. Memorize his schedule and "accidentally" bump into him at least three times a day. The way you look at it, the more he sees you around, the more he'll think about you.

b. When you two are IMing, ask him to hang out with you and your friends. He seems like he's into you, so why not?

c. Hope he keeps talking to you each time you see him.

5. When you're crushing on a new guy, which animal do you channel the most?

a. A lion—bold, on the prowl, and ready to pounce.

b. A pony—you start out cautiously but get bolder once you know he likes you back.

c. An owl—super-mysterious and hard for other people to read.

6. When do you start calling a guy your boyfriend?

a. After dating for about a week—what's the big deal?

b. After a month or so— you don't want to seem too excited.

c. Only after he calls you the g-word first.

7. The first time you meet a guy's parents, you:

a. Beg to see naked baby pictures of their adorable son.

b. Ask the usual small-talk questions about their family to get the conversation going.

c. Usually muster only one-word answers to all their questions. The whole experience is so awkward!

Scoring

He sees you and thinks:

mostly a's: Run!

You think, I like him, so why shouldn't I go for it? Being strong-willed can be hot, but when it's too obvious you're into him—and you create ways to be with him rather than let them happen—you could weird him out. You may also look desperate (even if you're not). So curb your enthusiasm a bit—subtlety can pay off!

mostly b's: Sweet!

You flirt, but you're not one to assume he's interested before he's given you some signs. Guys respond to your steady strategy because they get a chance to warm up to you at their own pace, and you're comfortable taking it slow too. Plus, they see you as a bit of a mystery, which they can't help but want to solve.

mostly c's: Who's she?

Being a lovezilla isn't your nature, but if you don't send any signals that you're into him, he'll never know! Your crush needs a bit of encouragement, since guys are just as scared of rejection as you are. (And sometimes they're just plain oblivious!) Start small: One little smile won't make him think you're in love with him. But it could cause a spark!

ARE YOU WRECKING YOUR LOVE LIFE?

Find out if you're building a good foundation for longterm love—or demolishing your chances at romance!

1. New school year, clean slate for love! What's your romance goal for the coming year?

a. To find a cute new boyfriend ASAP!

b. To find your soul mate.

c. To kiss as many hotties as possible! You only live once, right?

d. To have a fun dating life but not ever get your heart broken.

2. You're waiting for your friend to finish buying something at the mall when a cute salesguy strikes up a conversation with you. You:

a. Give him your secret "boyfriend potential" test. If he passes, you'll ask him to grab a bite with you and your friend on his break.

b. Decide he's not your type if he's a guy who goes up to girls at malls.

c. Flirt until he asks for your number. One more for your little black RAZR!

d. Chat a little to see if he's cool.

3. The last time one of your relationships ended, how did you deal?

a. You moved right into a new relationship. It's the best way you know of to get over someone.

b. It took a while for you to move on. You kept always comparing guys to your ex and finding things wrong with them.

c. Relationship? You haven't been with someone long enough to actually go through a breakup!

d. You wallowed for a week and then forced yourself to get back out there.

4. A friend wants to set you up with her hot cousin. So you:

a. Say, "Sure! When?" before she even finishes her sentence.
b. Stalk his MySpace to see if you're into the same bands and stuff. If his tastes are different, it's a no-go.
c. Ask her to invite him to a party this weekend so if you're not into him, you can flirt with the other guys there.
d. Just let things play out naturally. You might see him at a basketball game next week. If sparks fly, then great.

5. Which celeb's love life is most like yours?

a. Mandy Moore. She moves seamlessly from one serious relationship to the next.
b. Natalie Portman. She'd rather be single than casually date someone she's only sort of into.
c. Anne Hathaway. She has a ton of prospects and loves getting the eye of every guy in the room.
d. Keira Knightley. She knows love when she sees it and isn't afraid to commit when it's there.

Scoring

mostly a's: You're a serial dater

It seems like you're always in a relationship with barely any time off in between. Yeah, it feels good to be part of a couple, but make sure you're with a guy because you like him, not because you don't like to be alone.

mostly b's: You're overly picky

It's good to have high standards, but don't be so quick to shut out guys who aren't your "type." Try to open yourself up to connecting with guys who don't fit your first-glance criteria. You may find one who really "gets" you after all!

mostly c's: You're boy-crazy

Flirting with tons of guys is fun, but when you do take the time to get a feel for what it's like to connect with just one guy, you'll be part of a couple. And that can be just as much fun as playing the field.

mostly d's: You're in control

Your thinking is right on target. If love presents itself, you know how to recognize it and go for it. And if it doesn't, you have fun anyway. That open-minded attitude will lead you to a solid romantic future (no bulldozers in sight!).

DO YOUR BOYFRIEND'S FRIENDS LIKE YOU?

Are you an innie or an outie?
Discover your status within his group of friends.

1. When you interrupt your boyfriend and his buddies watching *Kung Fu Hustle*, they:

a. Turn up the volume and pretend they don't see you.

b. Mumble, "Hey," without looking away from the screen.

c. Offer you a spot on the sofa and a playful karate chop.

2. Your boyfriend is out of town and his best friend is throwing a party. Do you go?

a. No way. You weren't even invited—as if you care.

b. Of course! You're in charge of the late-night snacks!

c. Probably. His friends won't stop texting you to "Be there!"

3. You're stuck in a car with your boyfriend and his crew. Where do you sit?

a. In the driver's seat. You don't trust them at the wheel.

b. The middle backseat, so you're at the center of 'em all.

c. Shotgun! They really know how to treat a lady.

4. When you're giving your guy the silent treatment, his friends:

a. Take him out to meet other girls.

b. Play peacemaker—there's too much testosterone in the group without you around!

c. Say, "It sucks that you two are on the outs," then let you know they're available if you want to talk.

4. Which show's title best describes your relationship with your boyfriend's bunch?

a. *Dirt*
b. *My Boys*
c. *Entourage*

Scoring

mostly a's: No love lost

You and your guy's gang just don't mix. While that tension can be tricky for your boyfriend, there's no law that says you have to love his friends. As long as you let him have quality time with them sometimes, you can all share him!

mostly b's: But of course!

To your boyfriend's buds, you're more than just his girlfriend—you're their BFF too! But don't start scratching your junk in front of them—there's nothing cooler than a girl who can hang out with the boys without actually becoming one of them.

mostly c's: A little too much . . .

Aw! After spending time with you, the guys really like you—like, *like you* like you. But don't worry. When a guy's friends dig his girl, it only makes her that much more special to him. Just be very careful not to flirt with them—you're a one-guy girl!

WHAT'S YOUR KISSING I.Q.?

Time to enroll in Kissing U! Find out if you'll be an incoming freshman or P.H.D. candidate.

1. What's your idea of the perfect first-date kiss?

a. "Kisses" plural is more like it!

b. A sneak-attack smooch.

c. A sweet good-bye peck.

2. Have you ever practiced kissing on the back of your hand?

a. Yes. Practice makes perfect, right?

b. A couple of times, but not anymore.

c. Maybe once or twice, but I'd never tell anyone that!

3. What are you wearing on your lips right now?

a. Cinnamon-flavored lip plumper.

b. Shimmery lip gloss.

c. ChapStick.

4. What's the one thing you can't go without on a date?

a. Brown-sugar lip scrub—soft lips are sexy lips!

b. Peppermint Altoids—it's all about the breath!

c. Your best friend—double dates are more fun and less stressful.

5. Over-the-top, super-steamy love scenes in movies make you:

a. Swoon! You live for passion!

b. Warm and fuzzy. Especially ones with Jude Law!

c. Blush. Time for another popcorn refill!

Scoring

mostly a's: Phi Beta Kisser!

When it comes to kissing, you're at the head of the class! Your kissing M.O. is simple: Smooch well and smooch often, even if it's on your first date with a guy! As long as you keep things from getting too heated up, why not have a little fun?

mostly b's: Lip Smacker

Although you love to pucker up, you make a guy work for it! Sometimes this means you'll lock lips on the first date, sometimes not until the fifth. You wait until it feels right and when it is (whether it's sooner or later) the guy who gets to smooch you knows he's pretty special!

mostly c's: Smart Smoocher

To you, kissing is so intimate that the thought of it freaks you out a bit. But don't worry—if you're a snogging rookie, it'll just take time (and a sweet someone to practice with) before you're bumped up to the big leagues!

ARE YOU BITTER ABOUT LOVE?

Roses are red, violets are blue. Do you spread the love, or want to squash it with the bottom of your shoe?

1. Your school is selling roses for Valentine's Day. You order:

a. A dozen—all for your sweetie or crush.
b. One for each of your best friends.
c. None. That tradition is dumb.

2. Tomorrow is the 14th of February. You'll most likely be wearing:

a. A pink shirt, of course!
b. Whatever you pull out of your closet, but you accessorize with a heart locket.
c. All black, in mourning!

3. Okay, last V-day question, we swear! When you remember that Valentine's Day is coming up, you:

a. Are psyched—you love the holiday!
b. Don't obsess, but you do love those candy hearts!
c. Gag (What?! It's a reflex!)

4. You meet a cute, funny guy at a party and exchange numbers (score!), but he reminds you of your ex (sigh). When he texts you, you:

a. Arrange to hang out right away—new guy, new start!
b. Write him back and take your chances.
c. Ignore his message— what's the point, it'll never work.

5. When you pass the guy you like in the hall, your usual M.O. is to:

a. Run over and start chatting him up.
b. Smile and say hi.
c. Look straight ahead.

6. When was the last time you were really, really into a guy!

a. Right now. Actually you always are!
b. When you were dating your ex last year.
c. Not since you were 11!

7. You're going out with a guy for the first time. What's your plan?

a. Rent your favorite romantic movie.
b. Go bowling. It's kitschy and fun.
c. Who cares—you'll inevitably breakup.

Scoring

mostly a's: Sugar-coated

You see the world through candy-colored glasses. You're always open to love, but if you give it away too easily, there's a chance you may get hurt. Just be sure those you shower with love and affection do the same for you. Otherwise, keep being your sweet self!

mostly b's: Semisweet

You appreciate love and romance but realize it's not the answer to everything. That optimistic—but not overly obsessed—attitude helps you attract guys and it makes you open to relationships without feeling the need to listen to sappy love songs on repeat or bake pink cookies for your homeroom!

mostly c's: Bitter, much?

Your down-with-love vibes could block you from connecting with someone cool. Even if things went sour with guys in the past, it won't always be that way so don't shut them down before giving each new cutie a chance. Let your love life get a sugar rush at least once in a while and who knows, you might eventually end up with a sweet tooth!

WHERE WILL YOU MEET YOUR NEXT BOYFRIEND?

Find out where he's hanging out and go get him this weekend!

1. In the movie of your life, who would you cast as your leading man?

a. Shy James Franco.
b. Athletic Channing Tatum.
c. Intelligent Jake Gyllenhaal.
d. Cool Adrian Grenier.

2. For your next birthday, you definitely want to get:

a. A new laptop.
b. Portable speakers for your iPod.
c. An iPhone.
d. A vintage U2 tee.

3. What's your perfect dream date?

a. A romantic beach picnic.
b. Going insane at a Lakers game.
c. Browsing a new exhibit at a museum.
d. Being serenaded at an open-mike night.

4. It's Friday night, time to have fun! Where are you?

a. Watching *Grey's Anatomy*.
b. Playing laser tag with your friends.
c. Checking out a foreign flick with subtitles.
d. Flirting with the cute waiter at a coffee shop.

5. Which of these activities are you most likely to join at school?

a. Lit mag.
b. Varsity tennis.
c. Debate team.
d. Stage crew.

Scoring*

mostly a's: **On Facebook**

You're witty and introspective, but sometimes a little on the shy side. You like chatting online before you meet someone face-to-face. Send a message to the guy you friended last week and arrange a group date with all your pals. Before you know it, you may soon switch your status from "Single" to "In a Relationship."

mostly b's: **At a sporting event**

You're a bundle of energy and so outgoing that you seem to attract friends anywhere. Whether you're scoring the winning point for your team or just on the sidelines supporting your fellow athletes, everyone is routing for you (or with you!). So you're bound to find your love at the next big game . . . or he'll find you!

mostly c's: In class

You're so smart that you're always looking for interesting new ways to challenge your mind. Try putting your head together with the cutie in your class who may need help with a test coming up. Suggest a cozy cram session for two—and then be sure to take a few study breaks (wink!).

mostly d's: At a concert

From scouring thrift stores for vintage finds to filling your MP3 player with the latest indie groups, you're into doing your own thing. So when you're checking out that band you love, look around: There's a one-of-a-kind guy in the crowd who's ready to groove to your unique beat.

*Your type doesn't quite sound like you? Sometimes we choose what we want to be, rather than what we are. So take the quiz again with a friend who can help you pick the most true-to-you answers!

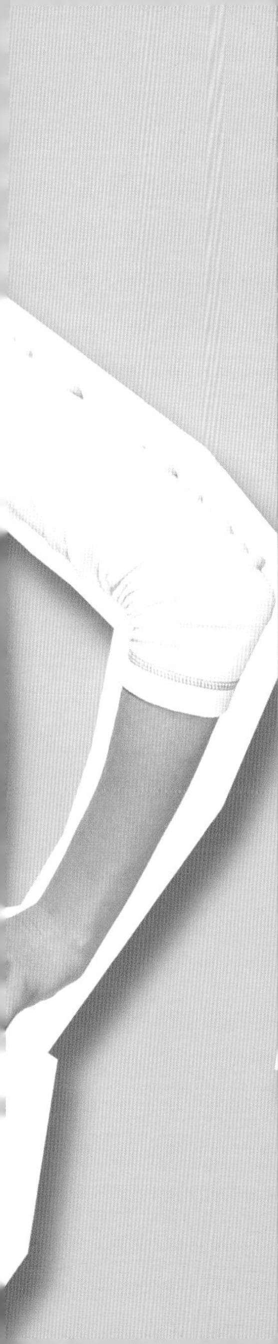

for fun

WHICH PAIR OF JEANS MATCHES YOUR PERSONALITY?

Like a tried and true friend, jeans will never let you down. Take this quiz to find out which pair is your perfect fit!

1. It's your friend's birthday. What do you get her?

a. Flowers, balloons, and a card.
b. You'll make her something special.
c. A chic pair of aviators.

2. If money were no object you'd show up to prom in:

a. A 1969 Mustang convertible.
b. A Toyota Prius hybrid.
c. A silver BMW M3.

3. Time for spring break! Where do you dream of spending the week?

a. Island hopping on a Caribbean cruise.
b. Exploring modern art galleries in New York City.
c. Scoping out the hottest boutiques in Paris.

4. What are you most looking forward to about going to college?

a. Being on your own, finally!
b. Having your own place to decorate.
c. Taking cool classes.

5. Your hair is usually:

a. Pulled back in a neat ponytail.
b. In some funky cut or style—you like to stand out from the crowd.
c. Flat ironed and sleek.

6. If you could bring along a celebrity pal to go shopping with you, it would be:

a. Reese Witherspoon.
b. Gwen Stefani.
c. Victoria "Posh" Beckham.

Scoring

mostly a's: Boot-cut jeans

You're a classic, just like a good pair of boot-cut jeans. Whether you're dressed up or going casual, you exude an easy-going, relaxed attitude. Your down-to-earth nature makes people feel comfortable and your friends flock to you for advice and support.

mostly b's: Customized jeans

You are a free spirit. No way would you conform to anyone's rules, and you've got the look to prove it. Whether you're embellishing your jeans with rhinestones, bleaching them out, or cutting them all up, you add your unique take on life to whatever you wear!

mostly c's: Skinny jeans

Like a great pair of skinny jeans, you are sophisticated and chic. Always one step ahead of the trends, people look to you for your sense of style. And you love to show it off—life is one big catwalk and every chance you get, you strut your stuff!

WHAT'S YOUR SECRET POWER?

You've got a hidden talent. Find it—and we'll tell you how to make money off it. Deal?

1. You're in a "good guys vs. bad guys" movie. Which good-guy role would you choose to play?

a. An FBI agent. You love to dissect clues and save the day!
b. An international spy. You'd do your own stunts, thankyouverymuch.
c. A cop (with a heart of gold!). Your gut always leads you to the truth.
d. A prosecutor. You'll make the bad guys play by the rules.

2. If your crush gave you a compliment (and why not? You deserve it!), which one would you be most likely to get?

a. "You're hot, and it's awesome that you're so smart too."
b. "You're hot, and I always have so much fun with you."
c. "You're hot, and you really get me better than anyone else."
d. "You're hot, and you give me the best advice."

3. Okay, admit it (we won't tell a soul!). What's your secret cable-channel addiction?

a. The Discovery Channel.
b. The Sci-Fi Channel.
c. A&E.
d. Lifetime Television.

4. At your best friend's party, you're likely to be:

a. Playing a game.
b. Dancing like a wild woman.
c. Having an intense conversation with just a few people.
d. Making yummy hors d'oeuvres.

5. You're doing a group project at school. You:

a. Volunteer to research it. You love surfing the Web.
b. Come up with really creative ways to present the topic to the class.
c. Know who's going to butt heads in the group, and play peacemaker.
d. End up doing most of the work since everyone else usually slacks off!

6. If there's one thing you can't stand, it's when you feel:

a. Like you look dumb.
b. Caged up like a zoo animal.
c. Betrayed by someone you love.
d. As useless as navel lint.

7. Your crush mumbles a message on your answering machine, and you can't understand him. You:

a. Play back the tape over and over and carefully consider the different reasons he might have called.
b. Call him back to find out what he wanted. What've you got to lose?
c. Call your friends and analyze why he might have called you.
d. Think his mumbling means he's nervous around you . . . which can only signify that he really, really likes you!

You're a . . .

secret strength: intellect

words to describe you: logical, strong-willed, innovative

power profile: You know that saying, "knowledge is power"? You're a sharp thinker, and your emotions don't get in the way of your decision making. You like to reflect on any experience to see what you can take away from it—whether it's good or bad. You think, "Okay, what did I learn and how can I use it in the future?" The result? Since you hate passing up opportunities, you tend to overload yourself and get stressed out. But your need to be in control whips you back on track.

how to work it: You're always thinking so fast that before you can put one idea into action, you've moved on to the next one. Make those ideas into success stories by strategizing! First, get yourself a special dream book, where you can jot down your interests and ideas. Soon you'll start to see that a basic interest in, let's say, travel, might morph into an idea for a teen travel guide. Whatever it is, it jumps out and says, "Pick me! You can do this!" Next: Own your idea. Plot out the steps to making it real (ask a teacher to help you write a book proposal, talk to a travel agent about getting free trips for research), and get started! That little book idea might get you a publishing deal and nationwide tour! Now, maybe you don't want to write a book. Fine—it's up to you to figure out what you'll do to make that dough. But if you follow this advice, it's only a matter of time before you will!

mostly b's: Free Spirit

secret strength: open-mindedness

words to describe you: unconventional, daring, optimistic

power profile: Some might call you a rebel, but you prefer "nonconformist." If the world didn't have people with "it's so crazy it might just work!" ideas like you do, there's no way we'd have cell phones, planes, or Napster. (Thanks!) But since spontaneity is your way of life, you tend to be a tad disorganized (just a tad!). Still, you're a charmer who everyone loves being around and who's known for turning even the most boring situation into a total blast.

how to work it: You can't just wing it when it comes to real success. The trick to making your multimillion-dollar ideas into real multimillions is the follow-through. So rally your entourage (you know, the people who'll be able to say they knew you when), and ask them to stay on your back about that goal you want to go after—whether it's Hollywood stardom or the dog-walking charity fashion show you dreamed up. Get a friend to help you create an action plan, ask another friend for her input, and so on. The more people who see you're serious about meeting this goal, the more people who will ask you if you've made any progress. You won't want to let them down, so you'll be motivated to keep at it. The bottom line? Marry your risk-taking ability with stick-to-it-iveness, because as the saying goes, "genius is 1 percent inspiration and 99 percent perspiration." If you follow through, there's no telling how much money you'll rake in. Um, can we have your autograph now?

secret strength: intuition

words to describe you: idealistic, sensitive, articulate

power profile: You're the ultimate people person. With your excellent listening skills, you "hear" what people aren't saying as well as what they are saying. (Psst! Your gut tells you!) Because you divide your energy among lots of people (you've got tons of friends), you sometimes end up putting your own goals on the back burner. Still, when you do dream, you dream big because you not only see what is, but what could be and what should be. It's a rare skill to have!

how to work it: How many times have you ignored your instincts and listened to someone else's advice? And how many times have you thought, "I should've gone with my gut!" Let that be your mantra, girlfriend. Use that amazing intuition to let your own personal truth lead you to your success. The next time you've got some life dilemma and friends give you their input, go spend time alone to reconnect with yourself. Write down everyone else's thoughts so you have them (after all, their advice doesn't always suck). Then pretend a friend came to you with this same problem. What would you tell her? That first reaction is what you should follow—even if you have to go against the grain. Whether you want to start your own magazine, direct a film, or do anything that makes someone ask, "How are you ever going to do that?" just know you'll find a way. People in high places will be impressed with your faith in yourself and put a nice paycheck behind it!

mostly d's: Guardian Angel

secret strength: maturity

words to describe you: responsible, supportive, organized

power profile: Okay, were you born grown up? You're the "put-together" girl who always keeps her head. So it's no wonder that you often find yourself being the plan maker! But by always taking charge, you sometimes end up resenting other people for slacking. Still, you really do love the fact that others feel safe with you around. Taking care of people makes you feel good.

how to work it: First, you've got to learn to let some things go. You don't have to be the one who does everything. But when something is really important to you—say, the planning of the prom—the key is to share the load. It's called delegating, and it's about you being the boss (like the sound of that?) and relying on others to do the individual tasks. By stepping back from the grunt work, you're in a position to make sure everything happens according to your very smart plan. The hard part is giving people orders in a way that doesn't make them feel like they're being bossed around. So instead of saying, "You should do blah-blah," try, "I'm thinking you'd be great at blah-blah!" Then, trust them to come through for you. If you give people stuff they'll be good at, you'll find they're psyched to pitch in. Once you master the skill of harnessing people-power, you'll meet your goals—and today and in the future!—much more quickly. And since managing people isn't easy, when you're a pro at it, you'll hear—"Okay, how much do you want to be paid?" *Cha-ching!*

ARE YOU PARANOID?

Find out if you have a tendency to freak out for no freakin' reason!

1. You're taking a biology test that's graded on a curve. You:

a. Tilt your desk away from everyone and write super-small.

b. Keep your answer covered with your arm.

c. Think, Who'd ever cheat off of me? Cheaters never win!

2. New semester, new locker combo. Where's the tape it was on?

a. Torn up and thrown in separate trash cans.

b. Somewhere hidden safely at home.

c. Tucked in the back of your daily planner.

3. You're walking home at night and hear steps behind you. You:

a. Run like hell.

b. Glance around to see who it might be.

c. Don't even break a sweat.

4. At the mall, you could swear people keep checking out your butt. You assume:

a. You have a big period stain on your tush.

b. That they must be looking at your cool shopping bag from that new store.

c. They're admiring your hot new pants.

5. Some guy comes up to you on the street and says, "Hey, aren't you a model?" You think:

a. Nice line, Bozo.

b. Wow! Your new haircut must look great!

c. Omigosh! How sweet!

6. When your teammates say, "Great job!" after the game, you think:

a. I must usually *really* suck.

b. I know I can do even better next time.

c. It's cool they're happy for me.

7. You get a voice mail saying, "Call back to claim your free trip to the tropics!" You think:

a. "Pshh—scam city."
b. "Too bad it's probably not real. A free trip would have rocked!"
c. "Cool! Free vacation!"

8. Your boyfriend seems quiet. He must:

a. Be mad at you.
b. Have something on his mind.
c. Not feel like talking.

Scoring

mostly a's: Completely paranoid

Chill, sister! Full-blown panic attacks regularly = bad. Everyone is *not* out to get you . . . or are they? Just kidding. They're not. We promise!

mostly b's: Wisely skeptical

Your inquiring mind could be onto something. You look at all the facts and make realistic clusions. Next stop: *CSI: Miami!*

mostly c's: Totally unsuspecting

Here on Earth, everything is not always as it appears. Watch faces, actions, and body language to get the real story.

WHAT DOES YOUR BEDROOM SAY ABOUT YOU?

Discover how your clutter can be a clue to your personality.

1. What does your bed look like on an average day?

a. Like it was devoured by your wardrobe.
b. Unmade with a few things on it.
c. Neatly made with pillows fluffed.

2. Quick! Where is your favorite pair of jeans?

a. In your room, flung over a chair or a lamp or something.
b. On the floor of your closet where you left them.
c. Neatly folded in your jeans drawer.

3. When was the last time you could see your floor?

a. Wait!? My room has a floor?
b. A few days ago.
c. You're looking at it now.

4. Your shoes are organized in your closet by:

a. Whatever direction you threw them in.
b. Season.
c. Color, season, and heel height.

5. Your new guy is coming over in five minutes. What do you need to do to get your room boyfriend-ready?

a. Hope for a miracle!
b. Make your bed, hang up some clothes, and straighten your desk.
c. Open the door for him.

Scoring

mostly a's: Miss Messy

You're laid-back and easygoing—and it shows. You'll clean when you absolutely have to, like when the laundry on the floor prevents you from opening your bedroom door! Your mess may drive your parents up the wall but it doesn't bother you one bit—you prefer your room to match your ultra-relaxed personality!

mostly b's: Organized Chaos

You've got your own system worked out—you know where everything is, even if no one else does! Having some order gives you peace of mind, so you'll straighten up when it gets too insane but you don't have time to go overboard—there are plenty of more important (i.e.: fun!) things you can be doing besides cleaning.

mostly c's: Neat Freak

Admit it—you have to stop yourself from cleaning when you're over at a friend's house! You're efficient and live by the motto, "a place for everything and everything in its place." Your room reflects this and being clutter-free is your key to staying in control—there's nothing worse to you than wasting time digging around in a mess!

WHAT KIND OF SANDWICH ARE YOU?

Everyone's hungry to meet someone new—but how appetizing are your ingredients?

1. If your life were a movie, it would be:

a. A romantic comedy.

b. A sub-titled drama.

c. An action-packed suspense.

2. Your perfect date outfit is:

a. A cute top and jeans—you feel sexy when you're comfy.

b. A new mini-dress—you love to wear something chic and flirty.

c. Lots of layers—you never know how you'll feel.

3. What does your usual weekend consist of?

a. Fri. with friends, Sat. with your guy, Sun. homework.

b. Divided between friends, family, and a little alone time.

c. Usual? Never! You're always doing something new.

4. It's your birthday! What's your ideal way to celebrate?

a. The basics: cake, dinner, a few close friends.

b. A party with tons of interesting, new people!

c. A trip to a place you've never been!

5. The best way to get a hold of you:

a. Just show up at your house!

b. Call your cell—you always pick up.

c. Send a text—you'll write back when you get a sec.

Scoring

mostly a's: The open-faced turkey melt

Like this yummy dish, what you see is what you get! You lay all of your feelings out on the table: If you're having a bad day, everyone knows it; if you like someone, you always let them know it. Being straightforward is great at times, but it may help your game to switch it up a bit and leave some things to the imagination.

mostly b's: The grilled panini

Your close friends know the real you, but when it comes to meeting new people you like to make them work for it! You've got an allure that keeps them wanting more and like this European 'wich, you're a bit sophisticated with just the right amount of layers to keep people guessing. Delish!

mostly c's: The monster club with everything on it

You've got so much going on in your head, people are never quite sure what might be inside—just like with this mega-meal! You're edgy and fun, always up for an adventure, and you love to keep everyone on their toes. A little mystery never hurt anyone, but sometimes it makes it hard for people to see the true you. So open up and let 'em know what it is you're thinking every once in a while!

WHAT'S YOUR MUSICAL MOVIE MATCH?

Admit it! You love to sing in the shower and dance around when you're alone. Give in to your guilty pleasure and see what big-screen musical you're meant to star in!

1. You're channel surfing after school, what catches your eye?

a. A dramatic/sappy Lifetime Original Movie.
b. A silly show on Comedy Central.
c. A steamy daytime soap.

2. What old-fashioned era had the best style?

a. 1950s—it was all about ladylike glamour.
b. 1960s—clothes were fun, colorful, and crazy.
c. 1920s—women dressed sexy but sophisticated.

3. Oh, man! There's an awful rumor about you going around school. How do you deal?

a. Write down your feelings in your journal.
b. Laugh it off—it's so obviously not true.
c. Start your own spicy rumor.

4. Your MySpace profile has tons of:

a. Meaningful quotes and lyrics.
b. Hilarious pictures of you and your friends.
c. Flirty messages from hot guys.

5. The best way to get your crush's attention is to:

a. Leave him a sweet love note.
b. Crack a joke that makes him laugh.
c. Lock eyes and subtly smile when you pass him in the hall.

Scoring

mostly a's: *Dreamgirls*

You're a romantic who is always daydreaming about how your life might turn out. Sometimes you can get lost in your own fantasies and just like Miss Effie White, it's your hopeful outlook on life that will help you dust yourself off when things get tough, and carry you on to sparkling success!

mostly b's: *Hairspray*

Like perky and positive Tracy Turnblad, you can be a little goofy sometimes. But people are drawn to your sunny, upbeat personality. Although you may act all fun and games, deep down you know you were meant to somehow make a difference in the world and always have an agenda ready to help get what you want!

mostly c's: *Chicago*

You love that people (especially guys) find you a little mysterious. There's an inner vixen inside you that would make Roxie Hart proud, but people have to know you really well to discover her! They'll have to break through your many intriguing layers, but once they meet your fun and flirty side, they'll find it was worth the time.

WHAT'S YOUR ROMANTIC MOVIE METER?

Take our trivia quiz to see if mushy movies make you cry tears of joy—or pain!

1. In *The Notebook,* how many letters does Noah write Allie?

a. 365, one every day for a year.
b. 364, once a week for seven years.
c. One, and then he stops when she doesn't reply.

2. In *Love, Actually,* where does the movie start and end?

a. Heathrow airport.
b. The Prime Minister's house.
c. Notting Hill.

3. In *High School Musical 2,* what does Troy give to Gabriella on the last day of school?

a. A necklace with a "T" for Troy.
b. His yearbook to sign.
c. The lyrics to a new song.

4. In *Enchanted,* who pushes Princess Giselle down the well?

a. Prince Edward's step-mother.
b. The dragon.
c. One of the seven dwarves.

5. In *Titanic,* where are Rose and Jack when they first kiss?

a. At the front of the ship pretending to fly.
b. Dancing below deck.
c. Exploring the luggage room.

6. In *Grease,* what sport does Danny get a letter in to impress Sandy?

a. Track.
b. Wrestling.
c. Car racing.

Scoring

mostly a's: Grab the tissues!

You're a chick flick champ! You feel the love (and heartbreak!) of romantic movies as if it's all really happening to you! Just keep those Kleenex nearby to dry your tears—and remember to take five from movies every once in a while and go create your own happily ever after!

mostly b's: Fast-forward to the good stuff!

You might not remember every line, but you love that warm and fuzzy feeling you get from watching a good romantic flick whether it's with your latest crush or just your best girl friends. Comfy couch, junk food, on-screen Prince Charming—that's your idea of a perfect Friday night!

mostly c's: Pass the popcorn!

Who needs fantasy romance when you can have the real thing?! You're much more into the cutie that's sitting next to you than the movie on the screen. You think that, locking lips with the leading guy in your life is way more appealing than an over-the-top movie kiss any day!

ARE YOU A BEAUTY DIVA?

When it comes to your beauty regimen,
are you a prima donna ... or a natural woman?

1. You have a big date tonight—and an even bigger zit. What do you do?

a. Reschedule and hide in your house until it's gone!
b. Cover it up with tons of concealer.
c. Relax—you doubt he'll even notice.

2. When was the last time you got your nails done?

a. The polish is drying as you take this quiz.
b. Less than a month ago.
c. For a special occasion, like prom.

3. Visualize all the makeup products you own. What kind of bag would you need to fit your entire stash?

a. A super-sized duffel bag.
b. A medium-size purse.
c. A mini clutch.

4. The paparazzi are waiting outside the drugstore to snap your pic. What do you do before leaving the store?

a. Hit the makeup aisle and feverishly redo your face using all the testers.
b. Slip on your shades and reapply your gloss.
c. Nothing, just head out, smile, and wave!

5. You snooze through your alarm the morning of a job interview. Do you make it on time?

a. No way—it takes time to look good!
b. Yes, but you had to do your hair en route.
c. Sure, you arrive bare-faced and early!

287

You're . . .

mostly a's: Diva-licious

Roll out the red carpet and grab that tiara—you're definitely in the running for the title of Queen Diva! Only your pillow knows what you look like when you first wake up and you'd never dream of leaving the house (gasp!) sans makeup. Just try to dial down the Diva every once in a while—even supermodels take days off!

mostly b's: A D.I.T. (diva-in-training!)

While running out of mascara wouldn't be your worst nightmare, you love to experiment with makeup and you like looking good. But you also know that there's a time and place to obsess over your hair and face. You may spend a lot of time getting ready for a big date, but you're also comfortable toning it down for, say, a game of ultimate Frisbee in the park!

mostly c's: The Anti-Diva

For you, diva is a four-letter word! You're a no-muss, no-fuss type of girl—a ponytail, a dab of mascara and a pinch of blush, and you're good to go. You'd much rather sleep in than spend loads of time in front of the mirror. Your fresh, natural, and never overdone look is the perfect match for your carefree, laid-back attitude.

WHICH WHITE HOUSE JOB ARE YOU DESTINED FOR?

Find out if you'll be hanging out in the Oval Office or somewhere else on the Hill!

1. Which one of these skills would make you a good detective? You:

a. Always create a plan of action.
b. Aren't afraid to confront and overcome obstacles.
c. Ask the right questions.

2. In kindergarten, you were known as the one who:

a. Wanted to be Simon in Simon Says.
b. Showed the other kids how to share.
c. Hogged Show and Tell time.

3. The prom queen vote is between you and your best friend. What do you do?

a. Run a tough but fair campaign.
b. Negotiate a deal to share the crown.
c. Talk up your friend but secretly hope to win.

4. When it comes to parties, you're the one who:

a. Insists on hosting them.
b. Makes sure they don't get out of control.
c. Spreads the word via Facebook.

5. A girl at school is spreading rumors about your friends. What do you do?

a. Stand up for your friends.
b. Confront the girl right away and get her to stop.
c. Clear things up on your blog.

Scoring

mostly a's: **President**

People can sense that you're a natural-born leader, and they know they can count on your master reasoning skills to conquer any challenge. Your confidence shines through in whatever you do. Better start practicing your State of the Union voice—there could be a real West Wing in your future!

mostly b's: **Secretary of State**

Being in the spotlight isn't as important to you as making sure everything goes smoothly behind the scenes. You're charming and responsible—you use your people skills to sense when something's off and then you get right in there to do damage control. As a result, people feel safe with you and look to you for advice.

mostly c's: **Press Secretary**

You're a great communicator. Anything sounds interesting when you're talking it up, whether it's a campaign to improve school lunches or a movie you want to see. When you talk, people don't just listen, they're convinced to act!

Discover Your Style

Fashion

Beauty

For Fun

fashion

WHAT'S YOUR STYLE VIBE?

Going shopping? Take this quiz to find out which style is right for you.

1. Your favorite amusement park ride *ever:*

a. The roller coaster.
b. The Ferris wheel.
c. The bumper cars.

2. You would name your dog:

a. Foxy.
b. Fifi.
c. Skip.

3. You'd be voted "Most likely to . . .":

a. Steal the school mascot.
b. Succeed.
c. Get married.

4. You'd blow $100 on:

a. Concert tickets.
b. A new haircut.
c. The perfect jeans.

5. Your dream wheels:

a. A motorcycle.
b. A convertible.
c. An old VW bug.

6. The sexiest J:

a. Josh Hartnett.
b. Justin Timberlake.
c. Jake Gyllenhaal.

7. Your lips wear:

a. Lipstick.
b. Lip gloss.
c. Chapstick.

8. Your must-see MTV show:

a. *The Hills.*
b. *Laguna Beach.*
c. *The Real Word.*

9. The best place to shop:

a. Forever 21.
b. H&M.
c. A vintage store.

10. You would take a plain white T-shirt and:

a. Rip it.
b. Rhinestone it.
c. Tie-dye it.

Scoring*

mostly a's: Wild

When it comes to fashion, you're way ahead of the game. You're always going through magazines and checking out the newest looks and you're not afraid to try something daring. Your friends admire all the wild looks you can pull off. No wonder you *always* stand out in a crowd!

mostly b's: Glam

You're stylish and self-assured. You're comfortable in your own skin and love glamming it up! Your fashion philosophy is all about playing up your assets in an elegant and sophisticated way. You'd be just as comfortable on the runway or red carpet as you would walking around the mall with friends, and it shows!

mostly c's: Vintage

You look back in time for style inspiration. Whether it's an amazing tie-dye shirt from your mom's closet or a beautiful brooch from your grandmother . . . you know how to make these looks work for you. You have a knack for taking something from the past and making it look current and fabulous!

*End up with a tie? Read both—it's like getting two for the price of one. Wink!

HOW FAR WILL YOU GO FOR FASHION?

Do you prefer to play it safe—or do you just play?

1. Your TV is always on:
a. MTV.
b. E!
c. VH1.

2. The coolest T-shirt you own is:
a. Studded and ripped.
b. Embroidered and cap sleeved.
c. Scoop neck and fitted.

3. Your most comfortable shoes are:
a. Metallic wedges.
b. Funky sneakers.
c. Ballet slippers.

4. When you're hanging with your crush, you want to look like:
a. A rock star.
b. A model.
c. Yourself.

5. You show up to family dinners wearing:
a. A miniskirt and halter top.
b. A cute cami and jeans.
c. A floral dress.

6. Your fashion idol is:
a. Paris Hilton.
b. Mischa Barton.
c. Mandy Moore.

7. Number one on your wardrobe wish list is:
a. A bright fedora.
b. A faux fur trimmed bomber.
c. A cropped peacoat.

8. You never leave home without your:
a. Cuff bracelet.
b. Fitted denim jacket.
c. Favorite cardigan.

9. On special occasions you wear your:

a. Black leather pants.
b. Little black dress.
c. Cashmere cardigan.

10. Your favorite lipstick is:

a. Sparkly orange.
b. Pink gloss.
c. Anything neutral.

11. Your fashion mantra is:

a. Shock 'em.
b. Dress to impress.
c. Less is more.

12. As far as book bags go, you'd kill for a:

a. Sequined hobo.
b. Leopard tote.
c. Leather knapsack.

Scoring*

mostly a's: Fearless Fashionista

Sparkles, glitter, wild colors—the more, the merrier! You're a fashion pioneer and you love being outrageous! And you don't care if someone looks you up and down. You've got it goin' on—and you know it. CG! fashion dares: try metallic pants or a denim micromini!

mostly b's: Fashionably Brave

Your philosophy: Always look done, but never overdone. If you pick a fierce animal-print top, you'll tone it down with a black skirt. Your unique spin on fashion has just the right amount of edge, so when friends follow your lead, you feel totally flattered! CG! fashion dares: leggings or a fringed sleeveless top.

mostly c's: Classically Cool

Trends are fun on the runway, but you're more into styles that hang around. You like timeless pieces, like great cardigans in cool colors and cute shoes that you can actually walk in. You, chic sister, always look fabulous because your kind of fashion is always in style! CG! fashion dares: black leather pants or a red cowboy hat.

*End up with a tie? Read both—it's like getting two for the price of one. Wink!

WHAT DO YOUR CLOTHES SAY ABOUT YOU?

Find out if your inner self and outer style match.

1. If you were a shoe, you'd be:

a. An aerodynamic running sneaker.
b. A simple leather boot.
c. A funky platform.
d. A skyscraper-high-heeled, sexy, strappy sandal.

2. The best place for a dinner date is:

a. A cozy little ethnic place with really cool music.
b. A classic bistro.
c. A chromed-out diner.
d. A fancy sushi joint.

3. What's your favorite get-up-and-dance CD?

a. Christina Aguilera's *Back to Basics.*
b. Fergie's *The Dutchess.*
c. Any great '90s album.
d. Beyoncé's *B'day.*

4. What outfit would your perfect date show up wearing?

a. Cargo pants and a cool hoodie.
b. Cords and a sweater.
c. Dark jeans and a Hawaiian shirt.
d. A leather jacket and beat-up jeans.

5. Which girl-power flick could you watch ten times?

a. *The Sisterhood of the Traveling Pants.*
b. *The Break-Up.*
c. *Pride and Prejudice.*
d. *Marie Antoinette.*

6. Whose closet would you most like to raid?

a. Kiera Knightley's.
b. Scarlett Johansson's.
c. Kate Hudson's.
d. Sarah Jessica Parker's.

Add 'em up!

Give yourself 1 point for each a, 2 for each b, 3 for each c, and 4 for each d.

6–10 points: Sporty and Stylish

If you can't jump in it or kick ass (not literally!) in it, there's no room in your closet for it. Your sporty, chic style reflects your sense of adventure. Play it up in: an old-school hoodie.

11–15 points: Classically Cool

You're all about the things that never go out of style, from little black dresses to comfy-cool khakis. Your sweet and smart clothes match your personality. Play it up in: a classic charm necklace or a super-luxe pair of perfectly fitted jeans.

16–19 points: Vintage-ly Hot

Your friends don't know how you do it: You walk into a thrift store, pick out someone else's old clothes, and end up with a look all your own. With your free-spirited personality, it's no wonder. Play it up in: boot-leg jeans and a sexy halter.

20–24 points: Red-carpet Ready

No doubt about it, Miss Trendsetter: From your ultra-glam hair accessories to your where'd-you-find-those heels, you're everyone's style idol. Play it up in: high-heeled ankle boots or a one-sleeved dress.

FIND YOUR FALL STYLE

You know that dream when you go back to school naked? Well, take this quiz quick and that won't happen to you!

1. Getting ready in the morning takes:

a. Over an hour.
b. 10 minutes.
c. Under an hour.

2. Your celeb crush:

a. Orlando Bloom.
b. Nick Lachey.
c. Adam Brody.

3. Pick a workout:

a. Yoga.
b. Tae bo.
c. A long bike ride.

5. Your dream tattoo:

a. Heart on your lower back.
b. Tribal chain on your arm.
c. Butterfly on your ankle.

6. Your dream vacation:

a. Touring a foreign city.
b. Camping and hiking.
c. Major beach time!

7. The best place to shop:

a. Urban Outfitters.
b. Niketown.
c. American Eagle Outfitters.

8. Best movie wardrobe:

a. *Material Girls.*
b. *She's the Man.*
c. *Just Friends.*

9. A girl can never own too many:

a. Shoes.
b. Pairs of sneakers.
c. White T-shirts.

Scoring

mostly a's: **Trendy**

You always know the latest fashion trends and you look great all the time. If there's a look of the moment, you're on top of it! You've always got your eyes open for the "it" bags and shoes of the season. When you show up back at school, all eyes are on you to see what the newest styles are!

mostly b's: **Sporty**

You're totally into being athletic both on and off the field. Your style is super sporty. Your active lifestyle requires you to be able to go from school to practice without too much effort . . . and you like it that way! Your focus is getting back in the game after a long summer off and your style reflects that.

mostly c's: **Classic**

You look put together and amazing no matter what you wear! Your closet is overflowing with timeless pieces that are always in style. Trends don't affect your overall look because you find a way to incorporate them into your classic style. Whether you start the new school year off wearing your favorite jeans or a perfectly tailored button-down, everyone knows you'll look great!

WHAT SUITS YOU ON SPRING BREAK?

Find out if you're as revealing as a teeny-weeny Brazilian bikini.

1. You hear a juicy secret about a girl in school. You:

a. Tell all your friends immediately!
b. Make sure it's true before telling your best friends.
c. Ignore it.

2. The role you want to land in the school musical involves:

a. Belting out songs as the lead character.
b. Playing a supporting part onstage.
c. Working on the script for the actors.

3. On *Fear Factor,* you'd rock at:

a. Eating those disgusting, slimy insects—you're game!
b. Those outrageous challenges.
c. You would never be on *Fear Factor!*

4. After you hook up with your crush, you're most likely to:

a. Give your friend the play-by-play.
b. Tell one friend—and have her keep it under wraps.
c. Stay mum.

5. Your favorite takeout food is:

a. Thai—super-spicy!
b. Chinese—a little of this and a little of that (it depends on your mood).
c. Pizza—you found the best pie in town.

6. You're off to a big party on Saturday night. You wear:

a. Something tight—you've got it, so why not flaunt it?
b. A cute miniskirt.
c. Jeans and the first clean T-shirt you find.

Scoring*

mostly a's: **A bikini**

You aren't afraid to let it all hang out (so to speak), which is why you're best in a bikini. Your bold personality makes partying with you a blast, no matter what the occasion. We bet your spring break will be a nonstop fiesta!

mostly b's: **A tankini**

Like your tankini, you reveal just enough to be interesting, but not so much that you're over the top. And you know how to be discreet: You love to hear gossip, but you never spill secrets. Chances are your friends are fighting over who gets to be your spring break roomie!

mostly c's: **A one-piece**

You don't see why you have to reveal everything about yourself right away. Wearing a one-piece says "What's the rush?" You'll reveal your fascinating self one layer at a time! This intrigues guys—and keeps them trying to figure out what makes the mysterious you tick!

*End up with a tie? Read both—it's like getting two for the price of one. Wink!

WHO'S YOUR CELEBRITY STYLE INSPIRATION?

Preppy, punk, glam or girly. Find out your celeb style.

1. Your iPod would feel naked if it weren't loaded up with which kind of music?

a. The hottest pop and dance music.
b. Punk rock.
c. Pop and country.
d. A bit of everything—top 40, rock, reggae . . .

2. Oh, snap! The paparazzi just caught you walking out of your house. What are you wearing?

a. At least one soft or fuzzy item, like fur-trimmed boots.
b. A T-shirt that says, "What are you looking at?"
c. Your favorite low-rise jeans and tank top.
d. Cargo pants and a top that you made yourself.

3. When you open your closet, what's the general theme that pops out at you?

a. Everything looks so glam!
b. How many pieces of black clothing you own.
c. All your clothes manage to be comfy and cute!
d. Your wardrobe spans the entire rainbow.

4. At your 10-year high school reunion, you'll be remembered as the girl who was:

a. The most popular.
b. The troublemaker.
c. The nicest to everyone.
d. The most creative.

5. *CosmoGIRL!* is organizing a fashion show in your honor (sweet!). What will the models be wearing?

a. Feminine clothes with a red-carpet flair.
b. Edgy designs that show off your rowdy side.
c. Cute outfits that are a little bit country.
d. A playful mix of styles, from retro to supermodern.

Scoring

mostly a's: Jennifer Lopez

Like Jennifer, the creative force behind the girlie-glam clothing line Sweetface, you always look like a million bucks. You've got a weakness for luxurious fabrics—like cashmere, velvet, and fur—and accessories. You know how to wear enough bling to blow them away.

mostly b's: Kelly Osbourne

Kelly's no pop tart, and her Stiletto Killers clothing line is just as bold and edgy as her attitude. You share her passion for punk, but like Kelly, you like to sprinkle in some glam—such a fashion rebel!

mostly c's: Jessica Simpson

The Princy by Jessica clothing line is full of down-home country staples like cowboy boots and gingham shirts. Like Ms. Simpson, your outfits signal a girl-next-door sensibility mixed with a little Daisy Duke sexy!

mostly d's: Gwen Stefani

You never know what Gwen's going to wear next, and you share her unique, eclectic style. You have a knack for mixing colors and prints like a pro—and that's the spirit Gwen brings to her fashion line, L.A.M.B.

DO YOU NEED A STYLE SHAKE-UP?

Is your sense of style nodding off to sleep? Find out if you need a fashion wake-up call!

1. What makes your favorite jeans special?

a. They're soft and faded because you've worn them so many times.

b. They look great with any type of outfit.

c. How could you pick a favorite with a closet full of different washes, styles, and cuts?

2. When's the last time you bought new clothes?

a. More than a month ago.

b. Within the past month.

c. Um, you were shopping online about two minutes ago.

3. A friend invites you on a hike and suggests dressing in layers. You say:

a. "I never leave home without a hoodie!"

b. "I'll bring my new sweater—it's nice and cozy."

c. "Ooh, maybe I'll wear a mini-dress over my capri pants."

4. Where do you usually shop?

a. The same few stores that you know you can count on.

b. You have a few favorite stores, but if a new place opens, you'll check it out.

c. You're always looking for the cool new spots, online and off.

5. When you find a basic shirt that fits you well, you think:

a. "I wonder if it comes in other colors!"

b. "This would look great with a trendier skirt!"

c. "It's so plain. How can I personalize it?"

Scoring

mostly a's: It's time to shake things up!

When you know you look good in certain clothes, it's easy to get into a fashion rut. If you're always in jeans, try a skirt. Obsessed with your cowboy boots? For a few days put something else on your feet. This weekend try on the clothes you already own, but in different combinations. You might discover a new favorite outfit!

mostly b's: You're already shaking things up!

You read fashion magazines for inspiration, but you're not obsessed with following the trends. When you shop, you choose new items that work well with the clothes you already own. You're great at combining pieces in a new way and adding personal touches to your wardrobe. So don't change a thing—you already have a great sense of style!

mostly c's: What's with all the shaking?

It's your sense of style on unsteady ground! You mix and match your clothes in wild, unpredictable ways, and you're known for constantly reinventing your look. It's great to be creative with your style, but you don't want to seem all over the place. Instead, start with a few key pieces that look good on you, then add layers and accessories that enhance those pieces.

WHAT'S YOUR BACK-TO-SCHOOL STYLE?

How will you look when you hit the hallways?

1. Number one on your back-to-school wish list is:

a. The perfect shoes.
b. The perfect bag.
c. The perfect jeans.

2. Your most comfortable shoes are:

a. Sequined ballet slippers.
b. UGGs.
c. Your Pumas.

3. You would rather look like:

a. A singer.
b. An actress.
c. Yourself.

4. At school, you're *always* wearing:

a. Some bling.
b. Silver hoop earrings.
c. Jeans.

5. The most-used item in your closet:

a. Miniskirt.
b. Black shrug.
c. Fitted denim jacket.

6. Your fashion idol is:

a. Gwen Stefani.
b. Jennifer Aniston.
c. Jessica Biel.

7. If you've got $20 to spend at the mall, you're buying:

a. A cute cowboy hat! Yeehaw!
b. A sparkly belt.
c. A comfy, fitted T-shirt.

8. The coolest shirt you own has:

a. Rhinestones.
b. A big silver initial.
c. A Hollister logo.

9. Compared to your friends, you dress:

a. The BEST, of course!
b. Sometimes better.
c. Similar to your friends.

10. Your fashion sense tells you to:

a. Flaunt it.
b. Dress to impress.
c. Less is always more.

Scoring*

mostly a's: Fashion Diva

You lead the way when it comes to fashion and you love being shocking! And you don't care if someone stares at you. Actually, you kind of like it! You've got the guts to be outrageous and you know it!

mostly b's: Trendy Fashionista

Your mantra is to always be on top of the latest trends, but not too trendy. If you pick a peasant shirt, you'll tone it down with jeans. Your creative spin on fashion has just the right amount of class, so if your friends follow by example, take it as a compliment!

mostly c's: Classic Chick

You're into timeless styles that stick around. Trends are fun on the runway, but not the hallway! You like classic pieces, like great T-shirts in bright colors and cute jeans that you can always feel comfortable in. You look amazing because your kind of fashion is always in style!

*End up with a tie? Read both—it's like getting two for the price of one. Wink!

WHAT SHOULD YOU WEAR ON YOUR DATE?

Instead of tearing apart your closet and trying on everything you own, let this quiz do the work for you!

1. What kind of activity do you have planned?

a. You're going to a party or a concert.
b. You're going out to dinner or a movie.
c. You're doing something sporty (either playing one or watching one).

2. How sure are you that it's an actual "date" and not just a friend thing?

a. It's just you and this one other person. Sounds pretty date-like.
b. You're positive that it's a date.
c. Well, you won't be that surprised if other people show up.

3. You tend to feel flirty and attractive when you're wearing:

a. Something shimmery.
b. Something flowing.
c. Something casual.

4. How much jewelry were you wearing when your date asked you out?

a. A lot.
b. A necklace or long earrings. Nothing too flashy.
c. Just some little earrings or a ring.

5. When you first met your date, you thought he was:

a. Hot!
b. Sweet!
c. Fun!

Scoring

mostly a's: Go glam!

Show off your sparkling personality in clothes with a little bling! Know that outfit that makes you feel like a star? It's perfect for your date. Add a few unique accessories, and they'll double as built-in conversation starters if you and your date run out of things to talk about. ("Like my necklace? I got it on my family vacation to Colorado . . .") Heels are fine, as long as you're not breaking in a new pair.

mostly b's: Go girly!

A date's the perfect excuse to play dress up with the most feminine clothes in your closet. If you're not in the mood to wear a little dress, remember — the right shoes and accessories can make jeans perfectly pretty! Plan your outfit beforehand so you can add sweet necklaces or hair accessories for a creative finishing touch. When you go on your date, you'll look beautiful and comfortable as you show off your personal style.

mostly c's: Keep it casual!

Some dates require dressing up, but for this one, you'll want to dress down. Instead of a skirt and heels, think jeans and sneakers. You're living proof that it's possible to look stylish and sporty at the same time. Just be sure your sneaks aren't old and gray— comfort's good, but you still want to look cute!

DO YOU NEED A MAKEOVER?

Mirror, mirror on the wall, do you need style tweaks or none at all?

1. You tend to go shopping:

a. Every Saturday: The mall is your second home.
b. Usually a couple of times a month.
c. When your underwear gets holes.

2. You'd fit right in as an extra on:

a. *Gossip Girl.*
b. *One Tree Hill.*
c. *The Office.*

3. When you think of your love life, you'd say it's most like:

a. A taco—spicy and full of surprises.
b. A roller coaster.
c. The hold button on your phone—sort of in limbo right now.

4. What's in your iPod right now?

a. The latest hip-hop, pop, and punk rock.
b. Indie pop that may not be on the Top 40 list, but you love it.
c. iPod? You'd rather listen to the radio.

5. There's a super-formal party in two weeks. You'll wear:

a. New dress, new shoes, new makeup.
b. Your favorite dress, with a colorful sash.
c. Your party dress—it always works fine.

6. The best-dressed girl in school is:

a. Why, you—but of course!
b. Your fashion-obsessed friend.
c. Not sure—but it's definitely someone other than you.

Scoring*

mostly a's: Style direct dial

You're on top of all the latest clothes and accessories before anyone else is, and people always come to you for style advice. (Admit it: You were the first to tuck your jeans into your boots!) But watch out: Dressing to impress can sink other priorities—and your cash flow!

mostly b's: Style 411

You've got fashion in perspective and know how to update your wardrobe with a few new pieces each season so you don't blow all your cash. You'll wear your perfectly worn-in jeans from last year, but with a cute blazer and vintage T-shirt to keep them *au courant*!

mostly c's: Style 911

Style doesn't matter much to you—and that's great, because it means you're not caught up in the ways of the superficial world. But you still want to look your best, so try jazzing up your look a bit with some slouchy boots or a flowy top over a tank. You'll look and feel refreshed—promise!

*End up with a tie? Read both—it's like getting two for the price of one. Wink!

beauty

WHAT SHOULD YOU DO WITH YOUR HAIR?

Okay, girl, let's take it from the top!

1. When you think about your upcoming birthday, you think:

a. Pah-ahh-ar-tay!
b. Yay, presents! Wonder what I'll get.
c. I should start planning something soon.

2. When a waiter tells a silly knock-knock joke, you:

a. Immediately tell him a funnier one back.
b. Smile politely.
c. Roll your eyes. What is this, kindergarten?

3. Which celeb best matches your beauty style?

a. Nicole Richie.
b. Jessica Alba.
c. Kirsten Dunst.

4. At an amusement park, you're likely to be:

a. Riding the roller coaster—again.
b. Nervously getting on the roller coaster.
c. Holding your friends' stuff while they ride.

5. For a history report on your town, you decide to profile:

a. An old speakeasy.
b. A hotel where famous people stayed.
c. The rise of your city's top industry.

6. Your friends always call you when they need advice on:

a. Sneaking out without getting grounded.
b. Boyfriends.
c. Comparison-shopping for laptops.

Scoring*

mostly a's: Show your sauciness

color: Add temporary streaks in a bright color.

style: Braid or dread (these are permanent, so be careful!) random sections.

cut: Have your stylist use a razor comb to give you a spiky cut. Looks like these will make you look even bolder, so you'll wind up feeling that way too!

mostly b's: Flaunt your versatility

color: Face-framing highlights bring out your eyes—wow!

style: Try a messy bun (easy but cool).

cut: Brow-length bangs can be worn down for a dramatic look or pulled back when you don't want to deal. These make your 'do simple, and make life more fun.

mostly c's: Prove your seriousness

color: Get a gloss treatment to add shine without changing your hair's shade.

style: Make a low ponytail, wrap a chunk of hair around the band, and tuck it in—classy but also fresh.

cut: Face-framing layers soften any simple haircut. You'll look in control, but not overly controlled.

*End up with a tie? Read both—it's like getting two for the price of one. Wink!

FIND YOUR SUMMER BEAUTY PERSONALITY!

Summer is just around the corner! Take this quiz to see who you will be when warm weather gets here!

1. The singer you're most like:

a. Jessica Simpson.
b. Rihanna.
c. Kelly Clarkson.

2. Puppies, kittens or pot-bellied pigs?

a. Puppies.
b. Kittens.
c. Pot-bellied pigs.

3. You talk to your friends mostly by:

a. Cell phone.
b. E-mail.
c. Text messaging.

4. The best place to shop for hair products is:

a. The salon.
b. The drugstore.
c. A beauty supply store.

5. You whip out your hand mirror to:

a. Check your lip gloss.
b. See if you are sweaty.
c. Spy on the cute guy behind you.

6. You'd feel naked without:

a. Bronzer.
b. Waterproof mascara.
c. Glitter eyeliner.

7. You like your nail color to match your:

a. Outfit.
b. Activity.
c. Mood.

8. Your first words were probably:

a. "Charge it!"
b. "Will this take long?"
c. "Does this come in black?"

9. You're constantly looking for:

a. The perfect shade of lipstick.
b. Hot new sneakers.
c. Indie-rocker boyfriends.

Scoring

mostly a's: Girlie

You love to experiment with feminine and flirty styles that give off a sweet and innocent vibe. Your perfect summer look is rosy cheeks and lips that look like they've just been kissed.

mostly b's: Sporty

You're always on the go and want a quick and easy beauty routine so you can play more. A little blush or some eyeliner is all you need for a quick touch-up.

mostly c's: Rocker

You have a creative, edgy sense of style and you're not afraid to take risks with your look especially in the care-free summer! You experiment with everything from liquid liner to fake eyelashes—and always look fabulous!

WHAT'S YOUR PERFECT HAIRCUT?

You want a look that fits your personality, don't you? So find what that is, right here!

1. When you walk into a room, you want people to think "she looks so . . .":

- a. Hot!
- b. Fun!
- c. Pretty!

2. Could you get ready for a dance in five minutes if you had to?

- a. Ha ha!
- b. With time to spare.
- c. Hmmm, maybe.

3. Getting a trim every six weeks is:

- a. Too hard to remember.
- b. More like every few months.
- c. A must.

4. Your ideal bikini:

- a. Teeny string.
- b. Tankini.
- c. Mix & match.

5. Your favorite makeup:

- a. M.A.C.
- b. Revlon.
- c. Covergirl.

6. Your perfect man:

- a. Ashton Kutcher.
- b. Zach Braff.
- c. Jake Gyllenhaal.

7. Your after-school activities require you to:

- a. Flirt.
- b. Run laps.
- c. Lead a meeting.

8. Would you ever trim your own hair?

- a. Maybe.
- b. Sure!
- c. No way!

9. What's your mom always saying about your hair?

a. "Just don't let your grand-mother see you like this."

b. "Have you washed your hair this week?"

c. "Won't you take it out of that ponytail for once?"

10. What's your hair most damaged from?

a. Bleaching, dyeing, teasing, or styling.

b. The sun or pool.

c. Your straightening iron.

Scoring*

mostly a's: Long locks

For a wild and sexy mane, have long layers cut all over your head—they look great on any hair texture. Then, flip your head upside down when you blow-dry.

mostly b's: Cute crop

A shortish look like this means easy styling! Ask for a shaggy, shoulder-length bob. For more texture, have your stylist chop your ends with a razor clipper.

mostly c's: Classic cut

An all-one-length cut is simple but still super-femme. Have layers cut from underneath if you have poofy hair. Add brow-length bangs to accent your face.

*End up with a tie? Read both—it's like getting two for the price of one. Wink!

ARE YOU A MAKEUP JUNKIE?

*Find out if your habit is average . . .
or if you're totally addicted!*

1. Your face-cleaning supplies consist of:

a. Um, the shower water is enough.
b. A foaming facial cleanser.
c. Everything: cleanser, toner, blemish cream, pore strips . . .

2. When you go out at night, you bring:

a. Keys and cash.
b. Lip stuff.
c. A mini makeup bag.

3. What do you wear on your lips?

a. Lip balm.
b. Fruity lip gloss.
c. Lip liner and lipstick.

4. Do you keep a compact mirror handy?

a. Nope.
b. Sometimes, on special occasions.
c. Of course!

5. The rosy glow on your cheeks is from:

a. Blushing, because of a cute boy!
b. A fading self-tanner.
c. Your highlighting bronzer.

6. How long do you spend on your makeup in the morning?

a. Not even five minutes.
b. No more than 20 minutes.
c. More than 20 minutes.

7. You run into your crush and you aren't wearing makeup. You:

a. Say hi.
b. Chat, but casually dab on lip gloss.
c. Hide!

8. You curl your eyelashes:

a. Eeek! Never!
b. Only when you remember.
c. Every day.

9. You go makeup shopping:

a. Hardly ever.
b. Whenever your mom offers to pay for your stuff.
c. All the time!

10. You think makeup is:

a. Nice on special occasions.
b. A good tool for when you want to look good.
c. Essential for looking your best every day.

Scoring*

mostly a's: What makeup?

You're the kind of girl who washes her face and then you're out the door. But if you want to try a little something new, dab some Vaseline onto your brows, lips, and eyelashes to give them a little polish.

mostly b's: Just the basics

You like makeup as long as you can still look like YOU. Try navy liner applied close to your top lash lines to define your eyes without being obvious. And keep doing that glossy-lips-and-rosy-cheeks thing!

mostly c's: Beauty junkie

You pull out all the stops with your makeup and you're willing to get up early to make sure everything looks perfect. Try red lips, with simple eye makeup. You'll make a sexy—yet subtle—statement!

End up with a tie? Read both—it's like getting two for the price of one. Wink!

WHAT'S YOUR POUT PERSONALITY?

Lips were meant to get attention.
Find out what's best for yours and pucker up!

1. On vacation, you pack:

a. Twice as many outfits as days, a girl needs choices.
b. A few basic outfits and a couple of fun accessories.
c. Only the essentials—you want room in your suitcase for souvenirs.

2. When your best friend wants to go on a road trip with you, you:

a. Cringe at the thought of sitting still for hours!
b. Devise a driving schedule and make a mixed CD.
c. Pack up necessary items and head off in a familiar direction.

3. At an amusement park, you love to ride:

a. The ferris wheel with your crush.
b. The pirate ship.
c. The water ride/log ride.

4. When your boyfriend is sick or tired during the weekend, you:

a. Party with friends at a new dance club.
b. Spend Friday with your friends and visit him briefly on Saturday.
c. Spend the weekend at his house, cheering him up with soup and crackers.

5. When your best friend gets dumped by her boyfriend, you:

a. Take her out dancing!
b. Take her to a hilarious movie.
c. Buy her gummy worms and spend the whole night talking about it.

6. If you found $50 on the sidewalk, you would:

a. Treat yourself to something new, like snake-print boots.
b. Take a close friend out to a nice dinner.
c. Buy early Christmas presents for your family.

7. Your last boyfriend liked this about your kiss:

a. The mark your lipstick left on his cheek.
b. How shiny your lips looked after.
c. The flavor of it that only he knew about.

8. In your circle of friends, you're:

a. Planning fun activities, like costume parties.
b. Cracking them up with your impersonations.
c. Baking cookies for them.

9. To prepare for your final math exam, you:

a. Study a little throughout the week and cram right before.
b. Study with a group of friends.
c. Study all week.

10. Before your friend's big birthday party, you:

a. Spend hours getting ready, it's her birthday, but that doesn't mean you should look bad.
b. Spend time getting ready with your friend.
c. Don't spend much time getting ready, but help your friend set things up instead.

Scoring*

mostly a's: Bright pink lipstick

You pull off this tricky color with style and attitude. You know how to grab attention, but you're careful not to try too hard to get it. After all, you have better things to do with your time . . . like asking your crush out!

mostly b's: Sparkly lip gloss

You want a simple look, but gloss gives you a little extra touch. You don't like it when things get too complicated, but a little glam every now and then never hurt . . . especially if it's for a hot date.

mostly c's: Fruity lip balm

You keep it simple and practical. Since you're on the go so much, you don't have time to worry about how your lips look; you just want to make sure they taste good at all times.

*End up with a tie? Read both—it's like getting two for the price of one. Wink!

WHAT'S YOUR PERFECT WORKOUT?

Know how your favorite jeans fit so well you feel like wearing them all the time? Well, your workout should be like that—so right you want to do it every day.

1. When working out, you like to sweat:

a. Not much at all.

b. Just enough to know you're working hard.

c. A lot.

2. When you feel stressed, you:

a. Meditate or take long, deep breaths.

b. Have fun with friends and try to forget about it.

c. Scream to release the tension.

3. What's your favorite part of working out?

a. Stretching: You find peace in feeling your muscles loosen up as you inhale and exhale.

b. Cardio: You like to feel your heart pump and know you're burning major calories.

c. Taking a class or doing a video: You feed off the energy of the music and the motivation of the instructor.

4. When you are in school, you:

a. Have no problem paying attention to the subject matter and sitting in your seat for the full 50 minutes.

b. Might get bored, but you power through it, taking notes because you know the work is important.

c. Need group activities or hands-on assignments to keep your interest.

5. If you were a Starbucks beverage, you would be a:

a. Chai Tea.

b. Skim Latte.

c. Java Chip Frappuccino.

Scoring

mostly a's: Pilates

You want to feel like you're toning your body and working your mind, but you don't want the huffing and puffing associated with most traditional workouts. Pilates is perfect for you because it's an effective but low-impact way to build long, lean muscles.

Mostly b's: Cardio-toning circuit

To you, exercise is a necessity, not a favorite pastime. That's why you tend to stick to a set routine, so you can do it and get on with your life. You'll love an efficient combo of cardio and toning, since you can get both done at the same time.

mostly c's: Sports drills

Energy's your middle name. And because you get bored with the same ol' routine, you prefer exercises that make you think fast and sweat. Your perfect workout is intense, with constant transitions from move to move, so you don't ever feel bored.

for fun

WHAT KIND OF PROM DRESS FITS YOUR PERSONALITY?

Discover which stylish getup for prom is just right for you!

1. What did you do last Friday night?

a. Baby-sat.
b. Hosted a *Sex and the City* DVD-athon.
c. Went to some older kid's all-night party.
d. Rallied a crew for some good karaoke.

2. If you could have their life for a day, which of these celebs would you want to be?

a. Reese Witherspoon.
b. Ashlee Simpson.
c. Katie Holmes.
d. Jennifer Lopez.

3. Which shoes do you like most?

a. Flat ballet slippers.
b. Stiletto heels with ankle straps.
c. Mid-calf black leather boots.
d. Pink UGGs.

4. Your ideal prom date would wear:

a. A classic dark tux.
b. A dark suit with a funky silk tie.
c. A coat and tails.
d. A hilarious baby blue tux— with a ruffly shirt to boot!

5. Your friends love you because:

a. You're always sweet and sincere.
b. You know how to make things fun.
c. You give the all-time best advice.
d. You'll try anything.

6. What do you sleep in?

a. Pastel-colored night gowns.
b. Perfectly broken-in T-shirts.
c. Matching top-and-bottom ensembles.
d. Nada!

Scoring*

mostly a's: Princess ball gown

You pride yourself on being a supergirlie girl! Sweet and cute, you're known for putting in the kind of extra effort that will always make you look classically feminine. You also appreciate and pay close attention to small details that others might miss.

mostly b's: Short cocktail dress

You're the life of every party! Carefree and confident, you make everyone feel comfortable when they're around you. Like your dress type, you're endearingly flirty and charming—and your spunky personality is infectious!

mostly c: Long, sleek gown

You're sophisticated beyond your years! Like this classic dress, you tend to be in the spotlight. But not because you're loud or clamoring for attention. Your quiet elegance speaks for itself, and that maturity and glamour attracts many people to you for advice.

mostly d's: Look-at-me dress

Your style is all your own! You have a natural knack for mixing and matching skirts and tops, combing thrift stores, and reconfiguring dresses to make them look totally new and unique. Some people think your eccentricity makes you too far out there, but that's exactly the reaction you want to get!

*End up with a tie? Read both—it's like getting two for the price of one. Wink!

WHAT'S YOUR WEDDING STYLE?

Take this quiz to see what kind of wedding you should have (in the very distant future!)

1. There's nothing like sliding your feet into a great pair of:

a. Ballet flats—adorable and so classy.
b. Heels. You look and feel sexy.
c. Flip-flops—they're just so darn comfy.

2. Your idea of a great plan for Saturday night is:

a. Going to dinner and seeing a movie.
b. Dancing at a club.
c. Having your friends over to bake chocolate chip cookies.

3. If you could shadow someone for a week, you'd pick:

a. A powerful politician or attorney.
b. The owner of the hottest new nightclub.
c. A holistic healer or an herbalist.

4. If you could have any car, it'd be:

a. A classy Lexus. It's sleek but practical too.
b. A flashy Porsche—people can't help but notice you in it!
c. An all-terrain Jeep to use for camping.

5. You win a trip anywhere in the world. You'd go:

a. To Paris to see the Eiffel Tower up close.
b. To the moon in one of those new expeditions for rich people.
c. On safari in Africa.

6. It's video night! You opt for:

a. A classic romance—you love tearjerkers!
b. A thriller—there's nothing like a good adrenaline rush.
c. An indie flick—the quirkier, the better.

Scoring*

mostly a's: Traditional wedding

You have great respect for time-tested traditions, and your wedding will epitomize your Princess Bride sensibility. For you, a perfect day would be planned all the way down to the last gorgeous detail (like the raspberry filling in your six-tier cake). Classic!

mostly b's: Las Vegas wedding

You think life should be a party, and what better place to hold your wedding than in Vegas! The way you see it, your time is too precious to waste by planning a gala affair, so you'd have way more fun getting wed by Elvis amid the bright casino lights!

mostly c's: Beach wedding

You're bohemian through and through, so why walk down an aisle when you can stroll through the sand? You prefer starting your own trends (like serving Chipwiches instead of cake) to sticking with the traditional. Your wedding will reflect that independent spirit!

*End up with a tie? Read both—it's like getting two for the price of one. Wink!

WHAT'S YOUR THEME SONG?

*Find out and belt it—
even if it's only in the shower or car!*

1. Friends rely on your ability to:

a. Give them the best practical advice.
b. Assure them that things will be okay.
c. Keep 'em laughing.
d. Make them think differently.

2. Your favorite after-school activity is:

a. School yearbook.
b. Volunteering in your community.
c. Playing sports.
d. It's different every day—you're just not much of a joiner.

3. You find a puppy! You name him:

a. Mr. Kitty—you love the irony of it!
b. Chance. Really, what are the odds?
c. Coffee—so hyper!
d. Bruiser. This one's a survivor!

4. You need music most when you:

a. Study for any big exam coming up.
b. Relax in a candle-lit bubble bath.
c. Work out.
d. Write or draw in your sketchbook.

5. Your report card is pretty disappointing. You think:

a. Darn, I should have studied more!
b. Next time, all A's!
c. At least I had fun this semester.
d. They don't get me!

6. Your friend flakes out again. You:

a. Think, Fine, and go back to your book.
b. Make other plans.
c. Head out solo—you'll run into friends.
d. Spill your feelings out on paper.

Scoring*

mostly a's: "How to Save a Life" by The Fray

Your song lets you focus your mind. You'd rather ponder life's deeper questions and be there for the people you love.

mostly b's: "Waiting on the World to Change" by John Mayer

You've always been a dreamer, and your song captures your hopeful essence—who knows what the future holds? You strive to experience life to the fullest.

mostly c's: "About Us" by Brooke Hogan

You love music you can move to. If it were up to you, life would be one big party (and for you, it's *already* started!). Your friends love your get-up-and-go attitude.

mostly d's: "Nothing in This World" by Paris Hilton

Music helps you get inspired! You're one tough cookie and you won't let anyone bring you down. Music helps you get out your frustrations and fuels your creativity!

*End up with a tie? Read both—it's like getting two for the price of one. Wink!

WHAT'S YOUR RINGTONE PERSONALITY?

Take this quiz to find out what your ringtone says about you!

1. If a company came out with a cell phone the size of a thumbnail, you'd think:

a. I have to get it!! I heard Paris Hilton loves hers!

b. I think I'll stick with mine. I'm used to it.

c. Cool! I wonder if I can shoot videos with it!

d. What if someone swallows it during a conversation?

2. Your birthday party is coming up next week. What are you planning to wear?

a. A trendy dress from your favorite online shop!

b. Your favorite skirt—you know you look great in it.

c. One of your own designs—you're working on it now.

d. Something unexpected, like a girlie dress with rain boots.

3. Before you clean your room, which of your stuff is causing the most clutter?

a. All your CDs, DVDs, MP3 players, and memory sticks.

b. Your favorite books and CDs, but it's still pretty neat.

c. Your latest art projects and all your art equipment.

d. Tchotchkes that crack you up, like bobblehead dolls.

4. You've finally managed to kick your brother off the computer. What's the first thing you check out online?

a. Your favorite celebrity gossip blog.

b. Your e-mail.

c. Your MySpace page, to see if your friends commented.

d. A humor site, like www.theonion.com.

5. History class is totally boring today, so you grab your cell phone and . . .

a. Change your ringtone— yesterday's is getting boring.

b. Send a text to your best friend.

c. Watch the iMovie you uploaded onto it.

d. Snap a pic of the guy who's snoring in the second row.

363

Scoring

mostly a's: A pop song

Whenever your friends need a pop culture fix, you're the first person they call. And with your impressive (and up-to-date) media savvy, it's no surprise that the latest *Billboard* hit (Chris Brown, anyone?) is your ringtone.

mostly b's: The standard

You're the classic, no-fuss type, so no wonder your cell (and its ring) isn't all tricked out. You care more about who you call than what you're calling with, so if the ringtone, um, rings, you see no reason to mess with it!

mostly c's: Your own creation

You always put a unique spin on everything you do, and your ringtone reflects that creativity. Whether you programmed in your own voice or the sound of a waterfall, you've invented something all your own.

mostly d's: A hilarious ringback

When people call your cell, they hear Napoleon Dynamite saying, "Are you gonna eat your tots?" Hilarious ringbacks like that perfectly fit your jokester persona. There's nothing that makes you happier than spreading the funny to your friends!

WHAT'S YOUR POWER GEM?

This quiz will "rock" your world—take it now to find the gemstone that will heal your soul!
To find the gem (or gems!) that's best for you, answer yes or no to each question as it relates to your life right now.

1.
Are you bickering a lot with friends and family?

_____

Do you often feel negative and hard on yourself?

_____

Do you feel stressed, afraid or frustrated? _____

2.
Do you have a huge test or paper coming up?

_____

Are you having trouble focusing or concentrating?

_____

Would you like to increase your mental clarity?

_____

3.
Are you trying to get over a bad breakup?

_____

Do you often end up in the wrong relationship?

_____

Are you having trouble getting over a crush?

_____

4.
Do you feel like you need spiritual guidance?

_____

Are you not sure what you believe in?

_____

Are you questioning your place in the world?

_____

Get your gem:

Match the category you have the most yeses in with its gem below.

1. Mother-of-Pearl

You need protection from negative energy. As its name implies, mother-of-pearl acts as a nurturer, absorbing negative vibes that may surround you. Wearing this gem will help keep you calm, give you a more positive outlook on life.

2. Blue Sapphire

You need brain food, and blue sapphire is the perfect nourishment! This gem brings order and clarity to your thoughts, so you can focus better. Wear it when studying for an exam or trying to solve a problem that requires serious concentration.

3. Ruby

Your heart has been broken or badly bruised, so ruby is the Band-Aid you need to wear! Ruby radiates a healing energy to help you recover from being hurt after a breakup or from unrequited love. It also gives you courage so you'll be ready to seek true love!

4. Amethyst

Wearing amethyst will guide you in your search for spiritual enlightenment. It promotes inner focus, helps awaken your soul, and make you aware of life's spirituality. This gem will help you connect to the world and discover your inner self.

FIND YOUR PERFECT PERFUME!

Know how one whiff of scent can take you back to another time? Our quiz will help you find one that'll make you unforgettable!

1. After school, you're:

a. Eating fruits and veggies.
b. Glued to the Food Network.
c. Picking flowers from the garden.
d. Petitioning for recycling bins.

2. Your friends describe you as:

a. Energetic and active.
b. Romantic and passionate.
c. Practical and realistic.
d. Laid-back and easygoing.

3. The celeb whose style you love:

a. Fergie—sporty and fresh.
b. Angelina Jolie—spicy and hot.
c. Rachel Bilson—flirty and girlie.
d. Sienna Miller—rustic and clean.

4. Your favorite workout style/class:

a. Aggressive kick-boxing.
b. Calming yoga.
c. Flowy dance routines.
d. Adventurous hiking.

5. You go crazy for the smell of:

a. Orange, lime, or grapefruit.
b. Homemade cookies.
c. Your neighbor's gardenias.
d. Your freshly mowed lawn.

Scoring

mostly a's: Fresh

You're an always-on-the-go girl! Lively, citrusy scents will complement your sporty, fun-loving personality.

mostly b's: Oriental

Warm, spicy fragrances spark your passionate personality, making you feel hotter than a stick of Big Red!

mostly c's: Floral

You're sensual and emotional, so florals are for you. They'll make you feel like you're in your own rose garden!

mostly d's: Woody

You're nurturing, so earthy, light scents that make you feel natural and refreshed are best for you. Ahhh!

WHAT'S YOUR PERFECT POOCH?

It's not what bag you're carrying, but the cute little dog you're carrying in your bag! Take this quiz and find out what pooch will not only match your look, but will also mesh perfectly with your personality!

1. If your friends assigned superlatives, you would be:

a. Sweetest.
b. Class clown.
c. Best dressed.

2. You want your guy to:

a. Be dependable.
b. Make you laugh.
c. Look great.

3. After a long week, it's finally Friday! Your weekend plans include:

a. Something outdoors, maybe a hike or a day in the park.
b. Seeing the latest Will Ferrell comedy with your girlfriends.
c. Hitting the mall to shop till you drop!

4. Your favorite outfit makes you feel:

a. Comfy and ready for anything.
b. Quirky and unique.
c. Trendy and sexy.

5. What's your bedroom style?

a. Laid-back—it's a place to chill!
b. Wild—it's filled with lots of patterns and things you've collected.
c. Girlie Girl—you've decorated it with lots of pink!

6. If your friends had to pick their favorite trait of yours, it would probably be:

a. Your adventurousness.
b. Your goofball sense of humor.
c. Your amazing style.

Scoring*

mostly a's: Lab dance

You're a girl on the go! With your spontaneous attitude, a high-maintenance toy dog isn't right for you. Whether you're running, hiking, or swimming, a Labrador will be right by your side, not in your bag. Join Mary-Kate Olsen and Kate Bosworth and get a Lab to join you on all of your fun adventures!

mostly b's: Go Pug yourself!

You're such a jokester! Why not let your dog join in on the fun? A goofy little Pug will not only help make others laugh, but will have you in hysterics as well. Join Jessica Alba and Tori Spelling and get yourself your own little pugster.

mostly c's: Cha cha cha Chihuahua

You're one chic girl! You know what looks good on you and how to work it. Being the fashionista that you are, a tiny Chihuahua would complement your style perfectly and look great in that hot handbag you just bought! Join Hilary, Britney, and Paris as a proud owner of a cheeky Chihuahua.

*End up with a tie? Read both—it's like getting two for the price of one. Wink!

All About Guys

You

Him

Together

you

ARE YOU BOY CRAZY?

A little dash is fine—and fun—but just make sure you're not completely obsessed!

1. A guy who flirts with you in your physics class is going on the school white-water rafting field trip. You've never tried it before. You:

a. Sign up and find a way to end up on his boat.
b. Talk to him about what it's like before the big day.
c. Skip it—water activities just aren't your thing.

2. You're throwing a big party next weekend. As you make the plans you think:

a. "There will be so many cute boys to flirt with!"
b. "Maybe that cutie from the baseball team will come."
c. "Did I buy enough soda?"

3. While your algebra teacher is going over the homework assignment, you're thinking:

a. Maybe I'll go to lacrosse practice after school to watch all the cute guys.
b. I wonder if I could ever set up a study date with that hot guy in front?
c. Darn! I thought the answer to number 4 was b^2.

4. You're at a party talking to a friend when a very cute boy sits down on the couch next to you. You:

a. Turn and ask him a question so he can join your conversation, too.
b. Talk a little louder so, hopefully, he'll hear you and try to get in your conversation.
c. Move a little closer to your friend so he can't overhear what you're saying.

5. A perfect night out with the girls is going to:

a. A party you've checked out in advance to make sure there will be loads of guys.

b. The movies—bonus if you spot a few cuties from another school.

c. A friend's house with videos and snacks.

6. On the walls of your room, there are:

a. Countless pictures of hot rock stars and actors whom you dream about dating.

b. A few pictures of your favorite celebs and a poster of a Monet or some other cool painting.

c. Photos of a trip you took, a portrait of you and your friends, and maybe some movie posters.

7. At the mall you see two really hot guys. You:

a. Follow them around until you "bump" into them.

b. Ask them where Abercrombie is.

c. Act like you don't see them and keep shopping.

Scoring

mostly a's: **Guy Loco**

You're like a girl in a candy shop but instead of Baby Ruth and Hershey, the candy has names like Jason, Tom, David! But listen up sister: just like regular candy, you need to take guy candy in moderation or you'll get sick. To find a meaningful relationship, you'll have to stop sampling all the sweets and start figuring out what you're really looking for in a partner. When you focus on the traits you like in a guy (and not just that he is a guy) chances are much better that you'll end up with one who's a great match for you.

mostly b's: **Guy Smiley**

You are the queen of crushing! You flirt with the guys that you think are hot but you've got other things on your mind too (school, friends, family . . . busy girl!) so you don't make guys the focal point of your life. Your interests make you more interesting to guys so keep at what you're doing. When the right one comes along, you'll find time for him in your schedule.

mostly c's: **Guy Shy**

Love and romance don't take up much of your thoughts right now and that's a good thing, because you've got plenty of other stuff on your plate, right? Plus, it's easy to be a little leery of relationships when they seem to make life even more complicated. But you know what? Keep doing your thing—your instincts will tell you when a certain someone is worthy of fitting into your life. So trust your gut—after all, it's led you in the right direction so far!

ARE YOU READY FOR ROMANCE?

Find out just how prepared you are to be part of a pair.

1. It's almost prom time, and it seems like everyone has a date—except you. You . . .

a. Don't mind going alone. You'll hang out with your friends and their dates—and probably have more fun than you would with some random guy anyway.

b. Call that cute guy you met last week at your cousin's party and ask him to go.

c. Put your friends (and relatives!) on a date-finding mission. You'd rather babysit your nightmare-of-a-brat neighbor than go to the prom without a date!

2. You think guys are like . . .

a. Lipstick: It can take a while to find one that really suits you.

b. Summer vacation: They seem to show up just when you're really ready.

c. Shoes: A girl can never have too many.

3. Your family makes the *3rd Rock From the Sun* clan look normal. When it comes to bringing your new guy around to meet them, you . . .

a. Skip it—for now. If he's still around in a few months, you might reconsider.

b. Get it over with. It means a lot to you that he meet them, and there's no time like the present for an introduction.

c. Tell him you're an orphan. You will not give those weirdos the opportunity to scare away a perfectly good guy.

4. It's Saturday night. You've got big plans to . . .

a. Have a sleepover with a bunch of girlfriends. You'll listen to music, chat, and try out all your new makeup.

b. Go out with a group of good friends (girls and guys)—probably for pizza and a movie or something equally mellow.

c. Hit a major party. You'll dance and hang out—and hopefully meet a cute guy.

5. Your best friend's boyfriend tells you he wants to introduce you to his cousin. You . . .

a. Say "No thanks." Please— you'd rather stay home and watch Discovery Channel reruns than go on a blind date.

b. Ask a bunch of questions (Is he smart? What celeb does he look like?) and then decide. You don't want to waste your time if he's not right for you.

c. Say "Sure, why not?" It's worth a try.

6. When you watch *Friends*, the character you secretly envy is . . .

a. Phoebe. She'll go out with someone if she's into him, but she's totally cool with being single too.

b. Monica. It may have taken a long time, but she managed to turn an awesome friend into an even better boyfriend.

c. Rachel. Her ultra-flirty routine means she's so good at getting guys, she's never dateless on a Saturday night.

7. Your dream guy finally asks for your number. You . . .

a. Give it to him, but you won't hold your breath. If you don't hear from him, it's not the end of the world.

b. Give it to him and then wait around by the phone, fantasizing about how great your first date is going to be.

c. Give it to him—and get his too. If he doesn't call you tonight, you'll have your best bud call him tomorrow to scope out how much he really likes you.

Scoring

Give yourself 1 point for every a, 2 for every b, and 3 for every c.

17 to 21 points: Flirt alert

You've never (ever!) met a guy you didn't like! You tend to fall in love fast and hard. The problem is, you lose interest just as quickly. Sure, dating around is fun, but it's hard to find true love that way.

Next time you're head over heels, ask yourself: Are you in love with the guy or just with the idea of being in love?

12 to 16 points: Fit to be tied

You, girlfriend, are totally ready to be part of a pair! You know what you're looking for and you're willing to wait, but when you meet a guy who interests you, you're not afraid to go for him. To get a good thing going, though, keep your priorities (school, friends, and him) straight.

7 to 11 points: Single sensation

You're independent, and you know you can always have a great time with your friends—you don't need a guy for that. It's not that you never want a boyfriend—you know that one day you'll meet the guy of your dreams. But your solo status is working for you now. Keep doing your own thing. You never know when love will sneak up on you.

GET SET FOR LOVE

A few steps to take before you pair off:

- Get interested. B-ball? Books? Backgammon? Doing lots of things you enjoy will make you more fulfilled. That way you won't need to depend on a guy to make you complete.

- Buddy up. Plan some quality girls-only time (crank up the tunes and let the bonding begin!). Forgetting about guys for a while helps you remember how great you are on your own!

- Treat yourself. Pick some roses, bake some cookies, or splurge on a new lipstick when you're down. You don't need a guy to boost your mood.

HOW GOOD ARE YOUR GUY INSTINCTS?

Find out if your gut reactions are a sixth sense—
or just a stomachache.

1. You run into a guy whom you've had two dates with and he's out with another girl. You figure:

a. You've just started dating so you can't expect him to be exclusive with you yet.

b. He's obviously not interested enough in you.

c. You'll poll your friends and do what the majority of them think you should do.

2. A guy who just moved into the neighborhood starts hanging around a little more with you and your friends. When he asks you out, you:

a. Invite him to a party so you can get to know him better before having a one-on-one thing.

b. Go. If he likes you he can't be such a bad guy.

c. Blow him off. He's too smooth to be real.

3. On your third date, your guy says "I'm exhausted! I've been working at the mall all day." You say:

a. "Let's do something chill so that you can put your feet up."

b. "Maybe you should find a job where you're not on your feet all day?"

c. "At least you're making money! Now you can pay for dinner."

4. Okay, come clean . . . the thing that you like most about him is:

a. He always tells you how beautiful and smart you are.
b. Every girl in school wants him!
c. He's a challenge—if it's too easy, there's something wrong with him.

5. The intense talk at the lunch table today was all about how that girl in your class hooked up with that guy at a party Saturday night. When you first heard the news you said:

a. "I knew it!"
b. "I can see them together—maybe it'll work out."
c. "I had no idea!"

6. Your crush is in your Driver's Ed class and is sitting in the back seat when you accidentally park on the curb. He says, "Don't worry about it, I've done the same thing." To you that means:

a. "Don't worry about it."
b. "What I really mean is ohmyGod, I can't believe you just did that."
c. "I like you."

7. Your crush seems pretty cool but his best friend is really obnoxious. You:

a. Don't care because you have a good feeling about who he is and that's more important.
b. Figure your guy is a jerk deep down, too and move on.
c. Won't judge him based on who he hangs out with.

Scoring

mostly a's: **Right on!**

You sure are good at reading guys and understanding what they're really about. Since your instincts are so fine-tuned, when you meet a guy you can listen to your gut to find out if he's worth your time or not. Of course, don't let your instincts lead you to make too many assumptions before you get to know a boyfriend candidate. Sometimes people will really surprise you.

mostly b's: **50/50**

You probably have good instincts, but sometimes they lead you astray and you might ignore them when the guy is really cute. Paying more attention to that feeling in your stomach when something is a little off—that's usually a sign of a bigger issue and you should stay away. If you have a hunch that he's not good enough for you, then trust your gut. There are other guys out there who are!

mostly c's: **Not so good**

You're either not noticing any guy signals or they're on over-drive, giving you the wrong messages. Since your radar's on the fritz, here's how to fix it. Sit quietly and ask yourself, "What do I need in a relationship?" If you're stuck, think about what qualities you look for in a friend and go from there. For example, if it's important to you that your boy has a great sense of humor, don't even date one who doesn't. Once you've got a list—either literally written down or at least in your head—of what you do and don't like, you'll be able to spot those qualities in a guy. And that's the first step to honing your boyfriend sixth sense!

WHAT'S YOUR FLIRTING STYLE?

Find out how to aim those Cupid's arrows just right

1. You're at the movies, waiting in line at the snack counter, when you spot your crush with some of his friends a couple of lines over. You . . .

a. Go over and flirt with his buddies. If all of his closest friends think you're cool, chances are your crush will too.

b. Go over to say hi, but chicken out and talk to another guy who's in one of your classes instead.

c. Look in his direction, and give him your sexiest Angelina Jolie pout.

2. Right now your biggest guy problem (if you had to narrow it down to just one) is:

a. You're getting a bit of a reputation, which is weird because you haven't gone out with that many guys.

b. Guys you're not interested in are always asking you out. But as for the guy you are interested in . . .

c. You've had a crush on this one guy for forever, and he still hasn't noticed.

3. What's the wildest, craziest thing you'd ever do to get a guy to notice you?

a. Wear an itsy-bitsy bikini to a pool party (even if you'd have to put up with a few stares).

b. Tell his best guy friend.

c. Start wearing his favorite baseball team's hat around school.

4. You're at the drugstore buying Aleve and tampons when you spot your crush—working behind the checkout counter! You . . .

a. Ditch the tampons, grab a CG! and some nail polish, and head straight to his line (even if it is the longest).
b. Duck and head to the pharmacy counter (in the back of the store) to pay there instead.
c. Put the tampons back, grab a box of those cute candy hearts, and get in his line. Maybe that'll send him a secret little V-Day message.

5. Your friend likes a guy she's friends with, but so far he hasn't noticed. When she asks for your best advice, what do you say?

a. "Flirt like crazy!"
b. "Just keep being yourself—he'll totally fall for you eventually."
c. "You've got to be subtle. Do you know what his favorite color is? Let's get you a shirt that color—that'll make him notice you!"

6. You're at your absolute most comfortable flirting with someone you like . . .

a. At a party, on the dance floor. That's where you can really let loose.
b. After a big pep talk from your closest guy friend.
c. In class—no talking's allowed, so you get to do all your flirting by shooting looks across the room.

7. Let's say you're out with a group of friends—and your crush—for dinner. What do you order to eat?

a. Your date's second-choice entrée. (That way, you'll have to share tastes . . . sneaky, sneaky . . .)
b. Whatever your best guy friend is having—he's got good taste.
c. Something exotic sounding, even if you secretly have no idea what it is. (You hope your crush will think you're really sophisticated.)

Scoring

mostly a's: Fearless Flirt

No doubt about it, you really know how to get a guy's attention. Only problem is, your crush can't tell you're into him if you flirt with everyone. Save your flirting for him alone, and make him feel special by asking him to dance or remembering his birthday. Our prediction: Pretty soon you'll be heading toward relationship-dom!

mostly b's: Accidental Flirt

It's easy to be accidentally flirty with guys who are just friends—they're safer than crushes! But don't you hate it when everyone's into you except your crush? Don't worry, it's an easy fix. First, try not to mislead guys you're not into. (Be nice, of course, just be extra careful not to flirt with them.) Second, tell yourself you're clearly a great flirt, and then flaunt that flirting confidence on your crush.

mostly c's: Subtle Flirt

Guys don't notice you like them, huh? Well, it's not because they're not interested. They just don't know you are! Face it, guys aren't great at getting subtlety. Simple solution? Be brave and turn up your flirting a notch. Flash him some slightly-longer-than-usual smiles in class. Or, if he's out sick, call him with the assignment. It may feel too obvious to you, but he'll just think you're super-sweet.

IS HE BOYFRIEND MATERIAL?

You already know he's totally hot.
Now discover his dating potential.

1. You realize that you'll both be at the Blink-182 concert on Friday night, and he suggests meeting up. When you finally spot him, he's . . .

a. Right up front in the mosh pit, sandwiched between two cute girls (with a third sitting on his shoulders!).
b. Hanging with a group of friends, saving you a seat right next to his.
c. Totally relieved to see you. He says he's been looking all over for you.

2. You're talking to him at lunch when your school's very own Jennifer Love Hewitt look-alike plops down next to him. He . . .

a. Starts acting like a smooth Mr. Cool—splitting his attention between the two of you and inviting you both to his big birthday bash next weekend.
b. Gets totally tongue-tied and forgets what you two were even talking about.
c. Says hi to her and then goes back to the conversation he's having with you.

3. He finally asks you out! But then your mom drops the bomb that she needs you to babysit your little brother that night. When you tell him the bad news, he says:

a. "That sucks. You're going to miss a really great party. Everyone'll be there."
b. "Can you try to get out of it? It's going to be an awesome party, and it would be way more fun if you were there so we could hang out a little..."
c. "Who cares about the party, anyway? How about if I bring over a couple of movies so we can just hang out?"

4. You run into him at a party after he said he couldn't go because he had to have dinner with his family. When you ask him about it, he . . .

a. Gets all weird and never really gives you a straight answer.

b. Says there was a change of plans and he totally would have called, but he couldn't find your number.

c. Says that dinner ended early, and he really wanted to see you, so he thought he'd stop by and track you down.

5. You're working together on a school project, and you've got a few weeks till it's due. He says, "I'll call you later to talk about it." He means:

a. "If you want to be remotely prepared for the project, you better get in touch with me before the due date."

b. "I'll try my best to call you later tonight, after I get home from watching the game with the guys."

c. "I'll call you tonight so we can watch Roswell together and then talk school."

6. You're at school and you lock your keys in your car. When you tell him your disaster, he . . .

a. Tells you he wishes he could help, but he's late for a jam session with his band.

b. Proves he really is super-sweet by offering to give you a ride home.

c. Acts as a one-man rescue squad: He finds a phone and calls the police, then waits with you (for an hour!) until they arrive to jimmy open the door.

7. True or false?

_____ He always wants to know what you've got planned for the afternoon/ weekend/ spring break/summer.

_____ You two are already friends.

_____ If you tripped in front of him, he'd help you up instead of standing there laughing with his friends.

_____ He'd be cool with it if you said your parents wanted to meet him.

_____ If you asked him for a favor (even a big one), he'd definitely come through.

_____ You feel comfortable hanging out with his friends, even if he's not around.

Scoring

Give him 1 point for every a, 2 for every b, and 3 for every c, plus 1 point for every true answer for question 7.

19 to 24 points: Just add girlfriend

This guy is exactly what a boyfriend should be—easygoing, generous, and fun. He's also a trustworthy friend and always there for you when you need him! Just don't make him the be-all and end-all of your existence. The truth is: Guys like you better when you do your own thing.

12 to 18 points: Pal with potential

This fun friend seems to be saying "I'm interested," so stay on the lookout for these signs that he's ready for more: He always talks to you when you pass in the hall and asks what you're up to after school. Remember, the best boyfriends started as just-friends, so try not to worry about your "relationship" status and focus on enjoying your time together instead.

6 to 11 points: The unsure thing

This ultracool guy is always the life of the party and a constant source of jokes. But if you look more closely, you'll see he's loving the single life too much to date just one girl. He'll grow up eventually, but for now, keep him in the just-friends category and set your boyfriend sights on someone who makes you more of a priority.

SHOULD YOU ASK HIM OUT?

Use these tests to read your crush's signals before you make any big moves. (Now, aren't you glad you keep us around?)

The Look Test

1. Looking straight into someone's eyes can reveal whatever feelings they have for you. Next time you two have a conversation, look directly into his eyes for a long count of three as you're talking (or as he's talking). When you try it, he . . .

a. Locks eyes with you, at least for a couple of seconds.
b. Looks away, and then looks back at your face (but not your eyes) and keeps up the conversation.
c. Looks away, gives fast answers, and ends the conversation pretty quickly.

The Prop Test

2. If a guy's into you, he'll be curious about your interests—that gives him something to talk about with you. When you're somewhere sitting by him (like waiting for class, or at the library), take out a sketchbook, read the liner notes of a CD, or flip through some photos. He . . .

a. Asks you about it and starts up a conversation with you.
b. Notices (out of the corner of your eye, you see him looking), but he doesn't say anything.
c. Doesn't seem to notice at all.

The Mirror Test

3. When someone's attracted to you, they may actually mimic your body language. By mirroring you, subconsciously they're saying that they relate to you. So, when you're sitting somewhere, change your body position (put your hand under your chin, or cross your legs) and see if he copies you. He . . .

a. Copies your stance almost exactly (down to scratching his nose when you scratch yours).
b. Eventually copies you.
c. Doesn't copy you at all.

The Food Test

4. Like kissing, eating is a mouth-oriented, sensual activity. So, when he likes you, he'll want to share something slightly intimate with you, like food. Bring something snacky to school (like pretzels, or homemade cookies). When he's nearby, just casually say, "Want some?" He . . .

a. Takes some and uses it as a jumping off point to start talking to you.
b. Either takes some and then turns away or says, "No thanks" but gives an excuse (like that he just ate).
c. Says, "No thanks" or nothing at all.

The Head-tilting Test

5. If someone's really listening to you (like, you know, someone who's interested in you), they'll tilt their head to one side as you talk. It shows that they're truly concentrating on what you're saying (and—here's the best part—that they care about what you're saying). So pay attention: The next time the two of you are somewhere talking, his head . . .

a. Is definitely tilted—a lot.
b. Tilts maybe a little bit off-center from where it normally would be.
c. Stays straight.

Scoring

Give yourself 3 points for every a, 2 for every b, and 1 for every c.

12–15 points: Project greenlight

He's definitely attracted to you. In fact, this guy seems so interested that the one big question is why he hasn't made a move on you. Make sure he's not already taken. (If he is, just be his friend for now.) But if he's free and clear, be bold. Call him for homework, ask him to prom, whatever level of flirting you're comfortable with.

8–11 points: Maybe, baby

Ooh, Mr. Mysterious! This guy is either interested and just shy or he doesn't think of you romantically (but he does want to be friends). How can you tell the difference? When you're talking, casually touch his arm for a second or stand close to him. If he doesn't move away or try to distance himself, you have our permission to flirt away!

5–7 points: Try again later

Sigh. He probably isn't interested in you right now. He could be into another girl or just not like your type (imbecile, we know). Or maybe he doesn't know you well enough. It's a risk, but if you want, get closer in baby steps: Say hi in the hall, and when you see him outside of school, be casually chatty. Once you're comfortable being his friend, try this quiz again. If he's still distant, drop him. Think of it as self pride: If he can't see why you're so loveable, he's not worthy of you!

WHAT DO GUYS SEE IN YOU?

You've got a certain something that makes guys adore you—so find out what it is!

1. A few guy friends ask you to join them for a Friday-night movie. You say yes and suggest seeing:

a. *Down With Love,* a romance.

b. *Phone Booth.* Colin Farrell in a psychological thriller with Katie Holmes . . . Sign me up!

c. *Bulletproof Monk,* a kung fu movie starring a comedian. Ridiculous? Definitely. Are you there? Definitely!

2. At a party, you meet a guy you've seen before— he's on the basketball team. You say:

a. "Hey, aren't you a starter now?"

b. "So how long have you been playing basketball?"

c. "Which was more hilarious: when the mascot tripped or when the ball bonked that guy on the head?"

3. Your lab partner is a huge flirt. When he goes, "I think we have some serious chemistry," you:

a. Wink and say, "Hmmm, I was kind of thinking the same thing . . ."

b. Roll your eyes in a friendly way and ask him whether he wants to measure zinc or take notes.

c. Make a joke right back, like, "Why? Do you want to get physics-al?"

4. At homecoming, a cute guy asks you if you want to dance. But your feet hurt, so you:

a. Ask him if he minds waiting for a slow song to come on.

b. Tell him that your dogs are barking and make conversation so he doesn't think you're blowing him off.

c. Hold off for a second and then get down anyway. Hey, it's called a dance, not a "stand around"!

5. One of your guy friends is totally overreacting about screwing up on yesterday's test. You say:

a. "Hon, was it really that bad?"
b. "Is something else bothering you?"
c. "Let's do something fun tonight!"

6. A class outing gets rained out, so everyone has to walk back to the bus through mud. You:

a. Cover your hair with your book bag and ask a guy for a piggyback ride.
b. Remind everyone to appreciate the zen of getting all muddy!
c. Trudge through the mud laughing and earn the nickname Mudhoney.

7. A big group is at a restaurant for a guy's birthday. You finally get next to the guest of honor and you:

a. Give him a huge hug and flirtatiously say, "Hey, birthday boy!"
b. Ask him how he feels now that he's another year closer to independence.
c. Tell everyone to hush up so that you can embarrass him by leading a hilarious toast.

You're . . .

Count up how many times you answered a, b, or c. Now read on, hot stuff!

mostly a's: Charming

After guys meet you, they think, "She's so hot!" But they're not (just) talking about your looks! You have a sweet, even flirty way of talking to guys, and that femininity draws them in. And it doesn't end there, girl! If you also show them what they wouldn't expect (like your love of Farrelly-brothers movies), they'll see the whole picture. Say cheese!

mostly b's: Sensitive

Guys may walk up to you with a clever pickup line, but they leave saying, "Geez, that girl is smart!" It's not that you're a mini Einstein (or maybe you are), but your thoughtfulness turns any chitchat into meaningful talk. Guys feel like they connect with you on a very intense, personal level. Just let them see your silly side too. It's genius!

mostly c's: Fun

Guys brag about you: "How cool is she?!" Maybe it's your humor or your casual style, but guys feel like you're one of them, and they love that they can just be themselves (bad jokes and all).

To make them feel truly special, also share when you're sad or serious. Then you'll have friends with potential for more.

WHAT TRAFFIC SIGNAL ARE YOU GIVING GUYS?

Learn the real vibe you're sending out.

1. The Shane West clone at school IMs you: "What's up Fri?" You:

a. IM: "Nothing—why? Feeling lonely?"
b. IM: "Not sure. Got plans?"
c. Freak out trying to decide what to do next.

2. Your cute neighbor jogs every day after school, so you:

a. Ask if you can join him.
b. Say hi when you go out to "get the mail."
c. Peek out your window every day at 4 p.m.

3. When you really like a guy, you:

a. Tell all your friends (and his).
b. Ask your close friends to help you figure out if he's interested.
c. Avoid him. If you talk to him, he'll know!!!

4. You consider it flirting when you see a guy in the hall and say:

a. "Hey sexy!" in a joking way, with a cute wink thrown in just because.
b. "I like your new shirt."
c. "Hi."

5. Your dating past is most like which celebrity?

a. Cameron Diaz—revolving door!
b. Jennifer Love Hewitt—you've broken a few hearts.
c. Natalie Portman—it's all top secret.

6. When a hot guy sits by you at a game, you:

a. Say, "Wanna have kids with me?" and hold out your Sour Patch Kids.
b. Ask which players he knows on the team.
c. Stare straight ahead.

Scoring

mostly a's. signal says: **Green Light**

You're advertising how much you want a boyfriend—and it's about as subtle as a forty-foot billboard. It's refreshing that you're direct, but the downside is that it might draw guys to you who just want to hook up. Figure out which guys on your list have real potential and focus on *them.* You'll be treated better in the long haul. Honk, honk!

mostly b's. signal says: **Yellow Light**

You flirt a lot, but sometimes guys can't tell when you really like them, so they wind up driving on by. (Boo!) There's certainly nothing wrong with talking to all the guys who interest you—variety is the spice of life, right? When and if you want to get serious, show your interest in a way that lets him know for sure you like him. You siren, you!

mostly c's. signal says: **Red Light**

Maybe you're still getting over a clunker of a guy or you don't know how to flag down your crush, but your flirting signals are more like stop signs. So if it's love you want, change your approach. Take it at your pace, but make a move—even if it's the first move. Next for you: cruisin'!

ARE YOU A GOOD DATE?

See if you're a master of the one-on-one night out.

1. You're supposed to go to a friend's party, but your date is in the mood to stay in and rent a movie. You:

a. Ask him if you can put in a cameo appearance at the party together and then go chill at your house.
b. Go to the party solo and then meet up later.
c. Tell him you really have to go to the party and cancel your plans with him.

2. You have plans for Saturday night, and he asks, "What do you want to do?" You answer:

a. "Maybe we can hit the arcade and then see a movie. Is there something you want to see?"
b. "Pick me up at 7 p.m. and I'll try to come up with something."
c. "Whatever you want to do."

3. You're on your first date together and things are going well but suddenly there's a lull in the conversation. You:

a. Ask about ultimate Frisbee (since you both play). Hey, this is your chance to get to know him. One lull won't stop you!
b. Show your date how you can balance a spoon on your nose.
c. Tell him you have an early class tomorrow—and call it a night.

4. Check please! Here comes the bill. You:

a. Suggest you split the tab.
b. Reach for it, but secretly expect your date to grab it and pay.
c. Head for the bathroom to avoid the awkward moment.

5. You notice that something green is caught in your date's teeth. You:

a. Say, "Um, you've got a little something . . . " and gesture toward your mouth.
b. Try as hard as you can to avoid staring at it.
c. Feel grossed out.

6. Date's over. You:

a. Kiss—but only if you like each other!
b. Wait to see if your date kisses you—then you'll know how the night went.
c. Quickly wave goodbye, and rush away from him.

7. It's the day after the date, you:

a. Wait one more day, then call your date to say you had a great time.
b. Call a friend to see if anyone has heard what your date thought of you.
c. Don't do anything. If he's interested in you, he should call you.

Scoring

mostly a's: Awesome Date

You really know how to make a date comfortable—you ask questions and flirt, plus you're sincere! While you've got this dating thing down to a science, we hope it's not because you feel that everything needs to be perfect. Because it doesn't. Believe it or not, sometimes the dates where you *don't* do everything right turn out to be the most fun!

mostly b's: Good Date

You've got dating skills, but you often feel like there's this point where you hit a wall and you don't know where to take it from there. It's tricky, true, but ask yourself how you'd want to be treated, if you were dating you (it's funny, but it works). Maybe you should turn up the flirting (looking into your date's eyes, touching him on the arm). It will give him cues for how you want him to act toward you, and that can help keep things progressing in just the way you want them to.

mostly c's: Date Potential

Feeling a tad nervous, are we, girlfriend?! That's totally okay—it's normal to be nervous for a date. Those jitters are part of what makes getting to know someone better so exciting. (But yes, it's scary at the same time!). Keep your cool by taking it slow and only do stuff that you're comfortable with (like going to the movies or out for ice cream). But keep in mind that he's just as nervous, and he'll be grateful if you suggest what to do or jumpstart the conversation. So try not to be afraid—just go for it and dating will get easier—and more fun!

CAN HE TRUST YOU?

Find out the truth!

1. Your guy tells you a secret about himself. You are most likely to:

a. Listen to him and take it to the grave.
b. Hint to your best friend that he told you something really juicy.
c. Call your best friend and blurt the story as soon as he leaves.

2. You're supposed to meet him at the mall at 3 p.m. It's about that time. Where are you?:

a. Standing in front of the food court—where else?
b. On your way—you're running late because a friend called as you were walking out the door.
c. Just waking up from a nap—oops!

3. Admit it—when Spanish class is really boring, you sometimes daydream about:

a. Your guy!
b. Ashton Kutcher—he really is hot.
c. The hot guy sitting in front of you . . . is he dating anyone right now?

4. He's off on a family vacation for spring break and he'll be missing some of the best parties of the year. When he gets back, you:

a. Tell him (and mean it) that it was no fun without him there.
b. Give him the full report, except for the guys who asked you out.
c. Will probably have a new boyfriend.

5. You're watching TV at his house and he decides to run out for pizza. While he's out you:

a. Go downstairs and chat with his Mom.
b. Open a few drawers looking for a pen . . . if you happen to stumble onto something else, it's just an accident.
c. Pour over each page in his notebook to find out if he has other girls' phone numbers.

6. Your guy admits that his last girlfriend cheated on him. You:

a. Are sad that he was hurt—you want him to know that you are faithful to him.
b. Think he suspects that you're seeing other guys too.
c. Wonder why he brought it up—does he think you're dating only him?

7. Your stance on flirting with other guys when you're going out with someone is:

a. You just don't even want to.
b. Depends on the situation. If your guy is around, then of course not. But if he's nowhere to be seen, then a little innocent flirtation doesn't hurt anyone.
c. Oh come on! I can flirt, I just can't touch!

Scoring

mostly a's: Solid Gold

He's very lucky to have someone like you. You don't look at other guys and you are really a friend to him and that's what makes a good couple. Being able to rely on you gives the two of you a foundation for a solid relationship. As long as he's equally as open with you and reliable, you're all set!

mostly b's: Gold-plated

You're usually open with him and try to be reliable . . . but sometimes it's hard to be 100% true blue. That's okay— relationships are hard and at this point in your life, it's important to put yourself first most of the time. But, if you want this relationship to last, then start building those trustworthy skills—no snooping around, keeping his secrets secret, and having eyes only for him.

mostly c's: Fool's Gold

Maybe there is something in the relationship that isn't right for you or you've been hurt in the past, but you're not the most trustworthy girl in the world. Your actions aren't showing that you truly care about the relationship, so you have to ask yourself why you're together. If you decide that he's the one for you, then start building that trust by being more open with him and keeping your word. There's still time to strengthen his faith in you.

DO YOU PLAY FAIR IN LOVE?

Find out if you're a good sport with your guy. Boyfriend or boytoy? Find out if you're being a bit too . . . well, manipulative, sister!

1. Prom is just around the corner and your guy hasn't said anything to you yet. You:

a. Ask him about it.
b. Hint about the big dance that comes near the end of the school year.
c. Start flirting with other guys to get yours jealous and light a fire under his butt—just in case.

2. You've been waiting for your guy in front of the school for twenty minutes. When you spot him, he's hanging out with his friends. You:

a. Walk over, say hi to the guys, and then say, "Hey, remember me? We were supposed to meet up?"
b. Pull him away from his friends to scold him for keeping you waiting.
c. Make a scene in front of his friends about how irresponsible he is.

3. When you and your boyfriend have a fight, you:

a. Take a time out, then you talk it out.
b. Explain to him all the reasons he should apologize.
c. Bring up an argument you had two weeks ago.

4. Your boyfriend is out of town, so you go to a party with the girls and a really cute guy asks you out. Naturally, you:

a. Say, "No, thanks, I have a boyfriend."
b. Avoid giving him your number, but keep talking to him.
c. Go out with the new guy—you haven't *exactly* agreed to stop seeing other people yet.

5. Your ex (who now lives far away) is in town and you have plans to get together with him. When your current boyfriend asks you what you're doing that night, you say:

a. "My ex is in town—I'd really like you to meet him."
b. "I might hang out with a friend."
c. "I'm seeing a movie with my sister."

6. Your guy calls on your cell phone and you ask where he is—he says at home, but you hear mall noises in the background. You:

a. Trust him—he's never lied to you before.
b. Wonder what he's up to—and call one of your mutual friends to see if he'll tell you where he is.
c. Run over to the mall to see if you can catch him in the act.

7. You like everything about your guy—except the way he dresses. You:

a. Don't really care—you adore him too much to care about tweaking these silly details.
b. Buy him a new pair of jeans as a present. Hopefully, he'll build some style skills with your help.
c. Sneak into his room, snag the most offensive items, and toss them out.

Scoring

mostly a's: Star Player

You always play fair because that's how you expect him to treat you. Just don't let your love of justice and compromise keep you from asking for what you really want or need. If you're ever hurt by him or just need some extra TLC, let him know. We bet he'll be more than happy to come through for you.

mostly b's: Fair Weather Player

When things are good between you, you think about his feelings while being true to your own. But when sticky situations come up—like when he does something you don't like or when another guy shows interest—you tend to skew toward what's best for you—and by any means necessary. Think about how you feel about your relationship. Learn how to work through things together. Like, if you're mad at him, instead of going behind his back to find out what's up or just trying to drop hints, be upfront with him. Use statements that start with "I." For example, "I felt like you were disrespecting me when you kept me waiting." That will show him that you know how to be fair and open with him while still being respectful of him.

mostly c's: Benched Player

Okay, here's a reality check—we hope it doesn't sound too harsh: you can't always be right and he can't always be wrong. But you act like that's how it is and it's not really getting you anywhere in the relationship. If you want this love to last, try to learn to see things from his perspective before you assume the worst. And try your best to stop lying to him to serve your own purposes—you wouldn't want him doing that to you, would you? Of course, if you just don't want to play that way, that's totally your prerogative. Just keep in mind that the best, lasting relationships are built on fairness, trust, and respect. Okay?

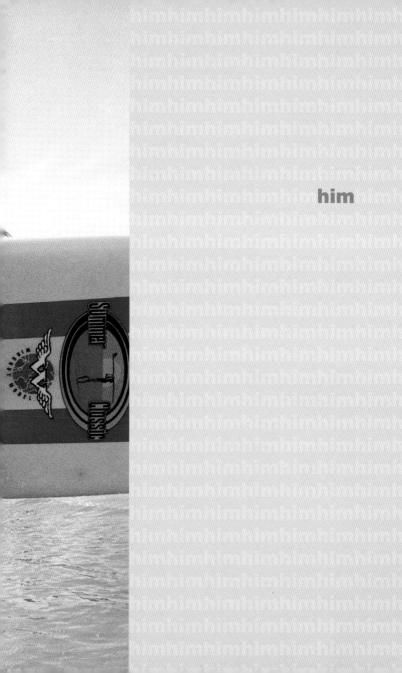

him

IS HE INTO YOU?

If he likes you, why doesn't he say something? Well, if you listen closely, he just might be trying to.

1. How much does your guy friend tell you about his dates: how they met, where they went, if they hooked up?

a. Absolutely nothing.
b. Some stuff, but it's all negative.
c. Everything—you're his confidante.

2. If the guy you have a crush on doesn't return your phone call, what does your guy friend say?

a. "I would never treat you like that! Why do you put up with that jerk?"
b. "That guy doesn't deserve you—you should be with someone who really appreciates you."
c. "Try e-mailing him—some guys aren't into talking on the phone."

3. When you answer the phone and say hello, which would he be most likely to say?

a. "Hi, Sweetie!"
b. "Hey, Superstar!"
c. "What's up, Stupidhead?"

4. Compared with his other friends, how close would you say you really are to him?

a. Soul-mate close. You talk about practically everything together.
b. Tight. You're definitely close, but you both have good relationships with the other friends—male and female—who are in your crowd.
c. Pretty close. But it's not like you talk on the phone every day or anything, like you do with all of your best female friends.

5. What inside joke do you guys have that he doesn't ever get tired of teasing you about?

a. How you two will totally get together someday.
b. The geeky guy you went out with (just once!) and the lame thing he kept saying during your date.
c. That time you tripped and fell right in front of the big windows at school.

6. How does his girlfriend (or a girl who likes him) treat you when you're in groups together?

a. She hates you! And he told you that she throws a fit whenever he hangs out with you.
b. You've caught her looking you up and down a few times, but generally she's pretty nice to you.
c. Like any other friend of his, girl or guy. You even hang out with her sometimes.

7. When you told him about your date with a guy you've had a crush on forever, what'd he do?

a. He listened for a minute, but then he said he had to go.
b. He made a sarcastic remark about how the guy was a player.
c. He was psyched but then wanted to tell you about the new P.O.D. video.

8. When you're hanging out with him, and nobody else is around, what's your "touch factor"?

a. He hugs you and seems to touch you a lot—on the shoulder, the knee, whatever, wherever.
b. He taps you on your arm when he's trying to get your attention.
c. He never really comes close to you.

Scoring

Give yourself 1 point for every a, 2 for every b, and 3 for every c. Now add 'em up.

8–13 points: **Signs say yes**

Hello?! He secretly throws darts at the pictures of any guy you like. So if you blush just thinking about him, then tell him that you're getting his vibe—he's just waiting for a sign that you like him back. Bring up the BF thing by asking, "People always seem to think we're together when we hang out? Wonder why?"

14–19 points: **Reply hazy, try again**

Things are getting warmer. Sure, it could just be his sarcasm that makes him trash your crush, but maybe it's more. So if you're interested, be like, "Yeah, let's see that movie, but want to go like a real date?" If he blows you off, be cool and say, "Joke!" It might be awkward at first if he says no, but knowing how he feels will let you stop wondering "what if" and focus on your friendship.

20–24 points: **Outlook not so good**

He doesn't seem to be into you in that way, and if you like him as more than a friend, that can hurt to hear. But you're still great together! He's someone you can count on to scare away losers, and you can always go to him for real guy advice. Consider yourself lucky to have such a fun friend whom you also really trust—that's nothing to sneeze at, sister!

WOULD I LIE ?

CAN YOU TRUST HIM?

Because let's be honest: Our hearts are sort of fragile. So find out the truth!

1. When you've made plans with him in the past, has he ever been late to meet you somewhere?

a. No, he's always insanely on time.

b. Yeah, once or twice, but he apologized and had a really good excuse.

c. Yes, he usually runs late, but he's just got a lot going on in his life.

2. Assignment: Sit near him at a time when lots of cute girls will be strutting their stuff (think halftime at a school basketball game or when you rent *American Pie 2*). How does he react to the babe factor?

a. He doesn't really pay attention—after all, he's too busy talking to you.

b. You notice him noticing them, but it doesn't go any further than that.

c. He's like a rottweiler faced with a poodle in heat—drooling.

3. You're going out of town and will have to miss Bridget's huge holiday party. On the night of the party, you'll worry that your guy:

a. Will be bored because you won't be there to hang out with him.

b. Will have a great and life-altering conversation with another girl—and even (who knows?) fall in love with her.

c. Will hook up with some (mean, crush-snatching) girl. Again.

4. For one whole week, secretly watch him at lunch in the cafeteria. Who does he sit with?

a. Usually, pretty much the same group of people every day.

b. A couple of different crowds of people. He switches off depending on his mood or who's in line next to him.

c. A completely different cast of characters, Monday through Friday.

5. Check out his homework ethics whenever your teacher collects big assignments. According to your research, he's the kind of student who . . .

a. Turns things in on time—always.
b. Procrastinates occasionally—but manages to get his assignments turned in about 80 percent of the time.
c. Turns things in—but only because he was able to copy off someone else's work in the hall seconds before class.

6. You say to him: "I have to be home by my 11 p.m. curfew." He says to you:

a. "Okay, then let's figure out an earlier time to meet so we have just as much time."
b. "Could you ask your parents if they will make it midnight instead?"
c. "Oh, come on—just blow it off. Your mom and dad will totally get over it."

7. How into his main extracurricular activity (whether it's a sports team, a school club, or a garage band) is he?

a. He's completely devoted to it. If there's a practice or a meeting scheduled, he's there no matter what.
b. He's active, but realistic. If there's nothing more important to do, he'll go.
c. If he wants to go, he'll go. If not, it's no big deal, he'll just skip it.

Scoring

mostly a's: **Absolutely**

Your guy is really respectful, and that's the key to trust. Need a ride? He'll show up—on time. Want to talk? He'll be there—in full support mode. We don't have ESP or anything, but it doesn't look like this guy would betray you. One catch: You have to be trustworthy too. If you're not, you could hurt him—especially since he's so earnest. So, be dependable, listen, and keep the private details of your relationship quiet. Congrats! We think you've found a truly great guy.

mostly b's: **Maybe**

We're kind of on the fence about him. Honestly, when you took this quiz you had some doubts, didn't you? So listen to your gut—it's probably right! Still want to give him a shot? Do the three-strikes test. Does he leave you waiting for a call? Strike one. Does he stare at a girl's chest? Strike two. Tell him specifically how you feel when he lets you down ("Waiting by the phone makes me feel like a loser—I could've been out with my friends"). He should work to earn your trust. If he doesn't, throw him out of the ball game, and sub in a better player.

mostly c's: **No way**

Yeah, he does that cute basset hound thing with his eyes. But should you trust him? Ehhh . . . nah. You've noticed that he misses commitments and breaks rules, and that shows that he's immature. Not to be harsh (look, we know it's tempting to likebad boys), but if you go out with this guy you may get really hurt. Look for someone who's more respectful (as in, an "a" category guy). Someone who respects you, won't cheat on you—and who you know you can count on. You deserve it, sister!

IS HE YOUR FRIEND...
OR YOUR FLAME?

Figure out if it's time to take it to the next level.

1. If you need his help with Brit lit, you:

a. Bribe him to come over.

b. Just ask, and he finds the time.

c. Don't say a word—he can just tell and he's on his way!

2. You two bump into his best friend, who says:

a. "Yo, weiner dogs!"

b. "Can I sit with you guys or is this a date kind of thing?"

c. "Are you two, like, married yet?"

3. During a DVD preview for a romance flick, he:

a. Hits "Skip Selection."

b. Gets up to go make popcorn.

c. Says, "Did you see that one? Maybe we should rent it."

4. At a party, you see him talking to a girl. He:

a. Calls you over to meet her.

b. Seems kind of uncomfortable for a second, then introduces you.

c. Drops her to hang out with you.

5. He always refers to your ex-boyfriend:

a. By his first name—you're all still friends anyway.

b. As "your last boyfriend."

c. As "Spawn of Satan."

6. After you win an "away" game, he:

a. Says, "Congratulations!"

b. Wants to hear all the details of your winning jump shot.

c. Leaps out of the stands to hug you.

Scoring

mostly a's: Fireless Friend

You've got yourself a true amigo here. You may be looking for more, but the comfort level you two enjoy is more
sibling than sizzling. But don't be sad—a friendship with
a boy is a valuable resource. Get his advice about your
other crushes—that's what guy friends are for.

mostly b's: Potential Flame

There could be a spark here, so if you want to try to light
it, you firebug, take a risk. Ask him to do something one-
on-one (like a "date") and see if he agrees. If it's not in
the cards, don't worry. True friends like you two will
always bounce back from that temporary awkward stage.

mostly c's: Serious Sparks

Did you really have to ask? You could have just looked
out on your porch, where your "friend" is probably waiting for you with chocolates! If you want him, it's up to
you to take his cues—because he's totally giving them to
you. Write him a note or grab his hand when you're walking with each other. Once you two get together, be ready
for some heat! (Tip: Buy a fan.)

IS HE USING YOU?

Find out what he really wants from you.

1. He talks you into going to a party you know will be lame and promises to leave in an hour. What happens?

a. Three hours later, you're dozing off in the corner, and he's still playing video games with the boys.

b. Exactly what he promised.

c. He checks in every two seconds to see if you're okay and then says he's ready to leave after a half hour.

2. A week before the big school ski trip, you blow your knee out playing indoor soccer. He:

a. Says, "That sucks" and asks if he can use your season pass.

b. Asks if you want him to stay home—and sends you postcards from the lodge once you convince him to go.

c. Cancels his spot immediately and uses the refund to buy you get-well-soon balloon bouquets every day.

3. You're hooking up, and he tries to take things a step further (again!). You say you're not ready, and he:

a. Sighs (like, "Oh, you're suuuuch a tease") and suddenly has to leave.

b. Apologizes for getting carried away and suggests you go for ice cream.

c. Starts sputtering that he hopes you don't hate him or feel pressured.

4. The two of you are in line at the movies when he realizes that he doesn't have any cash on him. He:

a. Does what he always does—waits for you to whip out a $20.

b. Asks if you can spot him this once.

c. Checks again and—aha!—finds the cash in his other pocket. He'd never think of taking you out unprepared.

437

5. Mr. Curfew Breaker can't use his car for a week, but he has to get to practice each day. He asks:

a. If he can borrow your car.
b. If there are any days you'd be in the area and could pick him up.
c. If you're mad he asked you to drive him to the bus station for a schedule.

6. He's coming over, and you ask him if he'll stop to get a soda for you on the way. He:

a. Arrives empty-handed—he "forgot."
b. Swings by 7-Eleven for a six-pack.
c. Brings you three kinds since he's not sure which you feel like having.

7. When he calls you after school, which of the following is he most likely to ask you?

a. "You coming over or what?"
b. "What's up?"
c. "Is there anything you need me to do for you? You sure?"

Scoring

Give yourself 1 point for every a, 2 points for every b, and 3 points for every c.

7–11 points: You're being used

In short, this guy thinks "girlfriend" means "someone who looks so cute fulfilling my every need." But you deserve to have your needs met too, girl. So the next time you want company on an errand or need advice, ask him for it. If he comes through, you've got a partner. If he doesn't, don't put up with a one-way boy. Unless you're a '77 Firebird, "used" is not cool. Okay?

12–16 points: You're being loved

Yes, he uses you—for friendship, fun . . . um, exactly the things you get from him. That's the way a good relationship works! But don't freak out when he needs extra support. It doesn't mean you're all about him; it means you're there for him. He'll be there for you, because that's just what good boyfriends (like yours) should do.

17–21 points: You're being needed

This may sound weird since he's so nice, but he is using you—to make himself feel needed. Basically, he doesn't like himself too much, so he works extra hard to get somebody else to. Show him you like him for who he is (you do!), not just for the stuff he does for you. And when he goes too far? Say gently, "Hon, I really like this gum, but you didn't have to buy me a whole case!"

WHAT KIND OF ROMANTIC IS HE?

He's your boyfriend, but where does he fall on the Prince-Charming-o-meter?

1. You're over at his house one day and notice that the first card you ever gave him is:

a. Next to other stuff you gave him—like a shrine dedicated to you.

b. On his bulletin board next to his track medal and family pictures.

c. Nowhere to be found . . . you're pretty sure he threw it out.

2. The two of you are about to walk out the door for a Saturday night date—he's springing for dinner at a fancy restaurant—when a torrential downpour starts. He:

a. Holds an umbrella for you.

b. Gives you his umbrella, and the two of you make a dash for the car.

c. Asks if you'd rather stay in and watch the WWE tag-team rematch.

3. Before you started dating he let you know that he liked you by:

a. Leaving a flower at your locker with a note that says, "This rose wishes it was as beautiful you are."

b. Spreading a rumor through his friends that he had a crush on you and then waiting for you to approach him.

c. Riding by your house on his bike until you noticed him.

4. In history class, he overhears you mention that you love poetry. He:

a. Composes an epic poem about the two of you.

b. Reworks the lyrics from an Eminem song that's sort of funny and sweet at the same time.

c. Teases you about it.

5. You and your best friend are in a really big fight. You know that you'll work it out but right now you're not on speaking terms. Your guy:

a. Writes you a note that says, "Don't worry—I'll be your best friend until she comes around."
b. Encourages you to talk things through with her.
c. Tells you she wasn't that cool anyway.

6. When you get a major part in the school play, he:

a. Sits in the first row of all five performances.
b. Comes to opening night and walks you home afterward.
c. Reads the review in the school paper.

7. It's your one-year anniversary. He'll probably:

a. Surprise you with a special date and promise ring.
b. Give you a card and take you to the movies.
c. Forget.

Scoring

mostly a's: Prince Charming

This guy knows how to make you feel special! He's *so* smooth that sometimes you wonder if he could be a player. Be sure that you are not so taken by his charm that you don't make an effort to get to know the *real* him. Ask him about himself, like "Where do you see yourself in ten years?" and "What was your earliest memory?" That way, you can get to know him instead of just letting him dote on you, and you'll build a deeper bond.

mostly b's: Charmingly sincere

This guy obviously likes you and knows how to romance you without going overboard. Being romantic back is the best way to let him know that you think he's a great guy, so try holding his hand first or buying him a cute card for no particular reason. He'll think you're even sweeter than he already does!

Mostly c's: Needs charm school

You may see his redeeming qualities and that's great—but admit it, this guy's got some learning to do! There's a good chance that he *wants* to be romantic but maybe he's afraid he'll look stupid. So try leading him by example: leave cute notes in his locker or plan a picnic—as long as you keep it private instead of public, he just might get swept up in the moment and get a clue for how to treat you to a little bit o' romance.

IS YOUR GUY A KEEPER?

These questions will reveal if you and the guy you're crushing on are ready for true romance.

1. What do your friends think of him?

a. He's cute! (They have crushes on him too.)

b. They think he seems nice but haven't really hung out with him.

c. They love the way he treats me.

2. Admit it, you still blush whenever . . .

a. I see him walk by me in the hall.

b. He makes a really flirty comment.

c. I accidentally burp in front of him (darn that soda!).

3. How often do you call him at home?

a. I've never gotten past dialing the first three numbers.

b. Whenever I can think of an excuse to ask him something.

c. At least once a day.

4. If your pet died (God forbid!), he'd:

a. Do nothing—he doesn't even know I have a pet.

b. Say, "I'm so sorry. Are you okay?"

c. Come over and make sure I'm okay.

5. Ever put his last name by your name?

a. Tons of times. Doesn't everybody do that?

b. Maybe once or twice.

c. Sure, and the two of us have even joked about it together.

6. When do you call him your boyfriend?

a. Just in my (locked and hidden) diary.

b. With my closest friends, as a joke—an inside joke.

c. All the time—after all, he is my boyfriend!

Add 'em up!

Give yourself 1 point for each a, 2 points for each b, and 3 points for each c.

6–9 points: Fantasy Find

Having a crush (a big, huge, heart-stopping crush) is so much fun—your smile gets bigger, your day gets brighter, and you've got an extra reason to look hot every day. But if you're too scared to really talk to this guy, you'll never find out whether it's going to turn into something real. Start by hanging out with him as a friend. Whether you end up liking him more or less in close-up, you'll finally be able to just be yourself with him.

10–14 points: Promising Prospect

Your guy is within reach, but for some reason, the fireworks aren't quite going off—yet. Maybe he's a friend or even an almost-boyfriend who can sometimes be kind of flaky. The fact is, he still gives you butterflies, so there's something real going on, just not quite full-blown love. Give things time to play out, and don't be afraid to have crushes on other guys in the meantime. You deserve someone who's just as into you.

15–18 points: The Real Deal

Romeo and Juliet. Jack and Diane. Brad and Angelina. You and your guy belong on this list of historically hot romances. It may not last forever (as in wedding bells) for you two, but you do know that one little fight won't end everything tomorrow. The good part of getting close is that you always have someone to talk to. Just make sure to spend quality time with your friends (separately) too. Lucky you (and lucky him!).

together

WHAT TYPE OF GIRLFRIEND ARE YOU?

These qualities aren't the kind of thing you should put on your resume, but it's good to know what category guys might be putting you in.

1. Today is your boyfriend's birthday! What are you doing for him?

a. We're going out for dinner before he heads out with his boys.
b. I've already brought him four gifts and made a cake.
c. Hanging out in one of our friend's basements like we always do.

2. When was the last time you and your boyfriend hung out, and what did you do?

a. We saw a movie together a few nights ago.
b. We're together right now. He's rubbing my shoulders while I take this quiz.
c. We went rollerblading together after school.

3. How well do your girl-friends get along with your guy?

a. They love him! Except for one girl. But whatever, it doesn't really matter what they think.
b. They don't really know him. I haven't spent much time with my friends since we started dating.
c. I actually don't have too many girlfriends—I get along better with guys.

4. When he says, "Go-Carts with the boys" you say:

a. "Movies with the girls."
b. "Call me when you get home, sweetie."
c. "Hang on, I'll grab my coat."

5. Your boyfriend calls you at 3:00 a.m., he can't sleep and he wants to talk. You:

a. Tell him to call you in the morning
b. Stay up all night long to talk.
c. Give him a few minutes, but boy are you tired.

6. The two of you are at the mall when he sees a micro mini in the window of Abercrombie. He asks you to go in and try it on, so you:

a. Put it on and laugh at how crazy short it is.
b. Buy it no matter how you look because he likes it.
c. Tell him that you would never even consider it.

7. You and he have had "the talk" and he has asked you to be his girlfriend and not see anyone else. You:

a. Tell him that you're into it as long as he respects that you do your own thing sometimes.
b. Exclaim, "Of course! You're the only one I want to be with."
c. Laugh and sock him in his side.

Scoring

mostly a's: The independent girlfriend

You love hanging out with him just as much as you are happy doing your own thing. The two of you have a great deal—you get to lead your own lives and you have each other to lean on for support. The fact that you have a world with friends and activities separate from his adds excitement to the time you spend together.

mostly b's: The sweet girlfriend

You are not afraid to tell him and show him how much you love him. Since you think in "couple" terms, you spend most of your free time together—or at least thinking of each other. You're the kind of girlfriend who is very involved in every aspect of your guy's life—and he totally digs that.

Mostly c's: The buddy girlfriend

Hanging out with the guys is your favorite extracurricular activity. You're the sort of girl who is happy to be with someone you can really pal around with. How amazing that you've got a fabulous friend and boyfriend—all in one!

ARE YOU HIS TYPE?

We figured you'd rather hear it from us.

YOU: Circle the letter next to the answer that best describes you.

1. What would you rather do on a Saturday night?
- i. Rent a movie with your best friend.
- e. Go to a club with lots of people.

2. Which English class assignment would you prefer?
- n. Write a three-page fictional short story.
- s. Write a structured three-page essay on any topic you like.

3. When you're annoyed with someone, what do you usually do?
- t. Confront them, and explain matter-of-factly why you're upset with them.
- f. Avoid them (or just avoid the whole issue that's got you all worked up).

4. If you could get back-stage passes to your favorite band's concert, but it would mean skipping a serious commitment (like playing in a semi-final bas-ketball game), would you?
- j. Yes, but only if you were able to cancel the appointment first.
- p. Yes. You could always explain later.

Okay, now write down the letters you circled for each question to get your personality LoveType:

_____   _____

_____   _____

HIM: Circle the letter next to the answer that best fits him.

1. When you see him around at school (like at lunch), he's . . .

i. Usually hanging out with the same couple of close friends.

e. Always hanging around with lots of different people.

2. Ask him what he would do if he won the lottery. He says he'd . . .

n. Do something creative (like start his own movie production company).

s. Buy something big, and save the rest.

3. Ask him what his favorite movie is and why. When he explains what he likes about it, he . . .

t. Talks mostly about the plot, the acting, or the special effects.

f. Talks mostly about how it made him feel ("It was a total rush"), or how he could relate to the characters.

4. Is he usually on time (to class, or to meet you or his friends)?

j. Yes.

p. No.

Write down the letters you circled for each of these questions to get his personality LoveType:

_____   _____

_____   _____

How it works:

Four traits determine your LoveType, which in turn affects your relationships.

Introverted/Extroverted Introverts love working alone. Extroverts are super-outgoing. Introverted guys tend to dislike extroverted girls.

INtuitive/Sensing N's are imaginative. S's are realistic. Matching couples communicate well.

Thinking/Feeling T's like making decisions with their brain. F's rely on their heart instead. F-girls and T-guys are the most common couple combo.

Judging/Perceiving J's like structure. P's are spontaneous. J/P couples fight over being late.

455

Scoring

Compare your results to score your compatibility.
Start with 10 points, then:

____ Add one extra point for every matching letter you both have.

____ If you're N and he's N, or if you're S and he's S, add six points.

____ If you're E and he's I, subtract five points.

16–20 points: Yes

You're totally his type. Whether you're friends or more, you just get each other. But even perfectly matched couples have some differences in their backgrounds or interests. Like if he loves extreme sports and you hate heights, he could help cure you. If you're too similar, you'll never change, and that's just boring. So be brave and cherish your differences!

11–15 points: Maybe

Big parts of your personalities are different, and that can be tricky. Survey says? Go ahead, try him, see what he's really like. If you can speak your mind even when your personalities clash (like in an argument), he might be a keeper. And if things don't work, it's not your fault—it's just your LoveTypes working against each other.

5–10 points: Probably not

It's not true love, but you could learn from him as a friend because he's so different. But to find your soul mate, think of what made you like this guy. Was it superficial? Abs are nice, but look deeper at future guys. Notice how he coos about his puppy or argues a point in class. Those peeks into his soul can attract you in ways that prove you're a good match—no quiz required.

IS IT LOVE OR LUST?

We sure are curious. Aren't you?

1. Be honest: What did you notice about him first?

a. His style.
b. His eyes.
c. His charm.
d. His thoughtfulness.

2. The word you'd use to describe your guy is:

a. Sexy.
b. Sweet.
c. Sensitive.
d. Soul mate.

3. If you have a bad day at school, you:

a. Go straight to Häagen-Dazs with your friends.
b. Stand by his locker—maybe you'll run into him.
c. Call his cell to talk and take your mind off things.
d. Go right over to his house—he'll be there to listen to every word.

4. You think about your guy:

a. When you're turned on.
b. During sixth period study hall (you know, when there's time!).
c. A lot, but not so much that you can't concentrate on real life too.
d. Practically every minute of the day.

5. At prom, you and your guy will likely:

a. Dance with other people but hook up afterward.
b. Be smoochy but not really talk about anything.
c. Hang out with friends but save all the slow dances for each other.
d. Stare into each other's eyes all night—come to think of it, was anyone else even there?

6. You and your best friends are talking about guys. When they ask what you love about yours, you brag about:

a. His body—there's simply no question.
b. His sweet smile.
c. His personality.
d. How well the two of you communicate.

Scoring

Give yourself 1 point for every a, 2 points for every b, 3 points for every c, and 4 points for every d.

6–12 points: **You lusty girl!**

Okay, so you like the way he looks, but deep inside that (muscular) chest of his beats a real heart (just like yours). Get to know it, and you may find he's even more special than you thought.

13–18 points: **Potentially yours**

Your vibes (and your lust drives) are in sync, and that makes things fun and meaningful all at once. You may not be super-committed yet, but if you're patient enough to get to know all the sweet and lovable things about him, this could last!

19–24 points: **So in love**

This guy just might be a keeper. You like the same things, you communicate well, and, best of all, you like each other's souls just as much as your bodies. But don't forget to make time for your friends (schedule dates with them too!). The more independent you are, the happier you'll be as half of a couple.

WHAT KIND OF KISSER ARE YOU?

1. When you have a crush on someone, what's your flirting style usually like?

a. Sexy and direct. He'd have to be blind to miss your signals.

b. If you're already friends, you'll tease him cutely. If not, you'll make friends with him first.

c. You take your time. You might be shy at first, but little by little you get closer to the object of your affection.

2. Cut an unpeeled orange into quarters. Put one of the four pieces in your mouth and try to eat the fruit off the rind. Stop after thirty seconds and take it out and look at it. What's left on the skin?

a. Nothing but white stuff—there's no fruit on the peel at all.

b. A little bit of mushy fruit.

c. At least half of the fruit.

3. How do you feel when you make direct eye contact with a guy you have a crush on?

a. More connected.

b. A little bit nervous—but a good kind of nervous.

c. Awkward, unless you already know the guy really well.

4. Ask a friend to time you: How many times can you say "red leather, yellow leather" in ten seconds? Ready, set, go!

a. 8 or more times.

b. 4–7 times.

c. 1–3 times.

5. Which of these three great movie kisses would you want to reenact? (And yeah, you can only pick one.)

a. Rhett Butler (Clark Gable) and Scarlett O'Hara (Vivien Leigh) in *Gone with the Wind.*
b. Wayne Collins (Greg Kinnear) and Jessica King (Katie Holmes) in *The Gift.*
c. Finn Bell (Ethan Hawke) and Estella (Gwyneth Paltrow) in *Great Expectations.*

6. Put on some bright lipstick, blot it once, and then give this box your best kiss! Okay, now take a look at your lip print. You can see:

a. A dark print of your complete top and bottom lip shape.
b. A lighter print of your lip shape that's slightly faded at the corners.
c. A light print of your lips that's faded in several spots.

7. Which word describes your ultimate, perfect kiss?

a. Steamy.
b. Frisky.
c. Romantic.

Scoring

mostly a's: **Passionate**

You're intense, and that kind of heartfelt emotion comes through in everything from your school essays to your Saturday nights out with the girls to (you guessed it!) kissing. Your kisses are fiery and powerful enough to make a guy forget his own name! Just make sure that you stay in control—if things start to heat up too fast, slow down and see how amazing just kissing can be. And if you're still waiting for that first kiss, know that it's going to be unbelievable!

mostly b's: **Playful**

Your close friends always talk about how honest and fun you are, don't they? Well, those qualities come from being confident, and that exact same confidence makes you an incredible kisser. Kissing you is like having a great conversation: Sometimes it's quiet, sometimes it's giggly, but it's always really comfortable. Whether you're considering kissing a new guy or about to have your first kiss, remember this: Only kiss guys you know, trust, and respect. That way, it'll be as real and perfect as you expect.

mostly c's: **Sweet**

If you've been kissing for years, or if you're waiting for your first smooch, you've got what it takes to make kissing tender and so romantic! You're a softy (admit it, sappy movies make you misty), and that sensitivity shows in your gentle kisses. You don't feel confident when you're kissing unless you know the guy really well, and that's good, because once you do kiss him, your vulnerable soft side comes out. *Hint:* A kiss on the nose will make him think you're even more adorable.

ARE YOU LOYAL TO EACH OTHER?

Are you hopelessly devoted to each other?

Instructions: The first five questions are for you and the next five are for your boyfriend. If you are not in a relationship, answer his questions based on a past relationship or answer how you think your crush would respond. Then see how loyal you'd be to each other.

Are you loyal?

1. Your boyfriend comes over, upset because he's fighting with his parents. But you're cramming for a chemistry final. You:

a. Take a break so you can hear him out. He's more important than studying.

b. Ask him nicely if he can let you finish and call him later.

2. Have you ever cheated on your boyfriend?

a. Never. You couldn't look at him in the face again after acting like that.

b. Oh, come on. Hasn't everybody?

3. You and your boyfriend are at the mall when a ridiculously hot guy walks by, obviously checking you out. What are you thinking?

a. "Is that guy staring at me?"

b. "Oh, yeah! *He* was staring at *me*!"

4. Which celeb's love life do you wish was yours?

a. Jessica Simpson. She has a genuine commitment and an adorable guy.

b. Cameron Diaz. She dates all the hottest guys!

5. What would you consider to be the ultimate Saturday night date?

a. Pizza and a movie with your boyfriend.

b. Going out with your girls and being hit on by several hot guys.

Is *he* loyal?

1. Your girlfriend comes over, she's in a panic but you just aren't in the mood to deal. So you:

a. Remember that she's always there for you and stop what you're doing.
b. Ask her if it can wait— you'll call her later.

2. Have you ever cheated on your girlfriend?

a. Never. You couldn't look at her in the face again after acting like that.
b. Oh, come on. Hasn't everybody?

3. You and your girlfriend are at the mall when a really hot girl walks by. What are you thinking?

a. "Is that girl staring at me?"
b. "Oh yeah! *She* was staring at *me*!"

4. Which celeb's love life do you wish was yours?

a. Nick Lachey. He has a genuine commitment and a sexy wife.
b. Justin Timberlake. He dates the hottest girls.

5. What would you consider to be the ultimate Saturday night date?

a. Dinner out at a fancy restaurant with your girl-friend.
b. Going out with the boys and hitting on girls.

Scoring

Calculate your responses separately—so you have a score and he has one. Each a is worth two points and each b is worth one point.

For each of you separately:

8 points or more: Loyal

You're devoted to this person because you truly want to be. Being faithful shows that you are very sure of yourself and you know what you want. It's not like you don't notice other prospects, but when it comes down to it, you know what qualities attracted you to him/her in the first place, and you know in your heart they're better than anything else you'd find in the dating pool right now.

7 points or less: A little fickle

Hmmm . . . we're sensing a one-sided relationship here, and that's not really healthy. Think about the reasons you first got together with the person you took this quiz with. Are those the qualities you look for in someone you're going out with? If you're still looking around, it may mean you want something different from what you have. If so, set this person free to find the love he/she is looking for—and deserves.

To rate your loyalty to each other, find the category that matches with both of your results.

If you're both loyal:

You sure are a tight duo! It's very special to find someone who believes in you as much as you believe in them. Keeping up this much momentum takes work, so continue to be respectful of each other's feelings and keep communicating—especially when you're upset with each other (even though that hardly ever happens, right?). Putting that kind of effort into your relationship will help you stay together for a long time. Sweet!

If only one of you is loyal:

Hate to say it, but your relationship is unbalanced. It might be time to get off the seesaw. Either the less loyal person must decide to make more of an effort to turn that less-than-dedicated behavior around, or it might be time call it quits. It's okay if the two of you just want different things right now—that happens in tons of relationships. But be honest with each other about what those things are, so you can decide if you want to try to start off on a new foot—or start walking away.

If neither of you is loyal:

It's time to have a talk about what you two really mean to each other. Your answers point to the fact that each of you is thinking more about yourself than about your coupledom. If this relationship isn't working, it's okay to break up—you'll both be happier when you don't have someone expecting something that you can't deliver. And if you part ways respectfully? Hey, you never know–maybe there's hope for you to try again in the future!

ARE YOU TOO INTO EACH OTHER?

If you have to let go of his hand to take this quiz, there's your answer!

1. Outside of school, you see him:

a. Every spare moment.
b. Mostly on the weekends, but once or twice during the week too.
c. Maybe once a week—when you don't have a party or something else to do.

2. At the end of his e-mails, he signs off with:

a. I love you, Sweetie-boo!
b. "Later," and his name
c. He doesn't—he just hits send.

3. You told him you love chocolate, but he brings you jelly beans (not your favorite). Your response is:

a. You don't really love me do you!?!
b. Thanks, that's awesome!
c. Thanks, I'll give them to my little brother.

4. You've been really busy with school and all of your after-school activities. Your guy:

a. Joins your clubs so that you can be together more.
b. Calls you almost every night to see how your crazy week is going.
c. Has no idea that you are involved in so many things.

5. Your guy calls and says that he isn't feeling well and doesn't want to go out. Naturally you:

a. Go over to his place with chicken soup and take care of him.
b. Make plans for when he feels better.
c. Have something else to do that night anyway.

6. When he picks you up at your house for a date, he:

a. Shoots some hoops with your brother, talks fishing with your dad, and catches up with your mom about her week at work.
b. Says "hi" to your family and then whisks you off.
c. Honks the horn for you to come outside.

7. What do your friends think about your guy?

a. They love him! But they sometimes wish they'd see you more without him around.
b. They really like him and seem cool with the two of you together.
c. They don't really know him because he and I usually hang out alone together.

Scoring

mostly a's: Too into each other

It's great to be so in love, but cupcake, you need to get back some balance in your life. Do you really want to spend every minute with him, or are you afraid that if you *don't,* you'll lose him? Here's the thing: it's dangerous to shut out other relationships with friends and family—a good pairing is tight enough to survive in the outside world. Try spending one night a week with your girlfriends and take up a new activity that has nothing to do with him—and encourage him to do his own thing a little more too. When you have your own things separate from each other, it keeps things more interesting—you'll have more to talk about when you do see each other. Ultimately, being secure on your own is what helps make you stronger as a couple.

mostly b's: Into each other

You guys are a healthy duo! You probably fell in love in the first place because both of you had a lot going on in your lives and that attracted each of you to the other. To stay on the same wavelength, keep supporting each other's interests—outside of your couple universe. If both of you stay true to yourselves and each other, you'll have the foundation for a great relationship.

mostly c's: Um, do you even know each other?

Don't take this the wrong way, but you don't seem all that into this relationship. It's fine to keep things casual so that he doesn't become the center of your life—in fact, we love that! But, if you ever do want to step it up with this guy, you'll need to make an effort. Plan some official dates, have a few marathon late night phone calls, that kind of thing. Spending some time and having deeper talks will bring you that emotional connection.

WILL YOUR LOVE LAST?

Feeling sneaky? Good! To see how long you and your boyfriend (or crush!) will be together, give him this secret test—he'll never even know he took it!

The Face-to-Face Test

Try out each of these tricky little scenarios on your guy and pay close attention to how he responds. Give him twenty-five points to start, then add or subtract according to these questions to find out how he scores.

1. Pass by him in the hall and give him a quick smile. He . . .

____ Sees you but just keeps walking. (Clueless jerk!) (-2)
____ Smiles back. (+1)
____ Smiles back and says hi! (+2)
____ Stops long enough for a quick conversation. (+3)

2. Check out how he acts in the lunchroom. He . . . (pick all that apply)

____ Laughs and/or applauds whenever someone drops a tray. (-3)
____ Sits at a guys-only table every single day. (-2)
____ Sits near you...but only sometimes. (+1)
____ Lets you cut in front of him in line. (Go ahead, ask him and see!) (+2)
____ Sets his tray (and his booty) right next to yours. (+3)

3. Show him a picture of your new puppy/car/baby brother. He . . .

____ Asks why you're showing him the picture. (-2)
____ Seems sort of interested. (+1)
____ Is really interested and asks you for details. (+3)

4. Give yourself one point for every time he initiates contact with you (a phone call, a note, a conversation) over the course of one week. ____

The Phone Test

Quick! Fill in these answers right after you hang up with him. Start with the score you had after #4 in the face-to-face test, and add or subtract as you go to get your final score.

5. Did he make you laugh?
____ Not at all (-2)
____ A little (but mostly because you were nervous). (+1)
____ Ha-ha-ha—Yes! (+3)

6. During your conversation, he . . .
(pick all that apply)
____ Talked about his ex-girlfriend. (-2)
____ Helped you figure out a problem (either homework or something personal). (+2)
____ Told you something about himself that you never would have guessed. (+3)
____ Yammered on and on and on about himself. (-3)
____ Asked your opinion about something. (+2)

7. Your conversation eventually came to an end because . . .
____ He had to go (but he gave you a decent reason). (+1)
____ He had to go (for no reason). (-2)
____ He took a call-waiting call. (-1)
____ You had to go. (+1)
____ It got late, and you'd both talked for so long, your ears were throbbing with phone-ache. (+3)

8. Give yourself one point for every two minutes you spent on the phone.
(A ten-minute call would be worth five points.) ____

Scoring

0–25 points: 1 month, max

Hate to say it, but your guy's not ready to be a full-time boyfriend. He's cute—just in an irresponsible, puppy-dog way. It's great if you guys talk, but if he's only blabbing about himself, he's not mature enough to care about you or a lasting relationship. Keep your eyes (and your Saturday nights) open for other crushes, and give this guy at least a year before you give him your precious heart again.

26–50 points: 2–6 months

You two will have ups and downs. That's a good thing. Whether he morphs into an ideal boyfriend or not, you'll have fun dating him. Plus, you'll decide what to look for in the next guy (a sense of humor) and what to avoid (a huge ego). You'll want to break up when you see that you can't make him perfect. Even if you can't date him now, maybe he'll be someone to come back to in the future. Test him again later and see!

51+ points: 6 months, plus

Hey, does your guy have an older brother? (Teasing!) He makes you laugh, shares his heart, and cares more about how you feel than if he looks "whipped" to his boys. Amazing! He's shown you what a good guy is like, so if you ever break up, you'll never settle for less. Just be careful not to ignore friends or your own goals. Boyfriend or not, you have to look out for you.

IS IT REALLY OVER?

Still hot for your ex? Well, find out if he is too, Miss Tabasco!

1. You invited your ex to come check out opening night of the new school play you're in. He:

a. Showed up and then waited around to congratulate you after the show.

b. Said he had plans but sent you a good luck e-mail the day before.

c. Just said he couldn't make it or didn't respond to your e-mail at all.

2. He showed up at a party with some girl you didn't recognize. When he spotted you, he:

a. Left her by the chips and talked to you for a good 15 minutes.

b. Introduced you two, then led her away to another group of friends.

c. Didn't seem to notice you were there; he was pretty into her.

3. During the first few weeks after you broke up, how many times did he call you?

a. A few nights a week, "just to see how you were doing."

b. Once, to find out the name of that old movie you both liked.

c. He didn't, and his buddy told you he deleted your number from his cell.

4. When you were together, he gave you his soccer jersey to sleep in. Since you've broken up, he:

a. Told you to keep it.

b. Has said nothing about it.

c. E-mailed you to ask you to give it back to him.

5. Since your breakup, his "boys," who you became friends with while you were together:

a. Still invite you to their parties and treat you the way they always did.

b. Will talk to you if they see you—as long as he's not around.

c. Have started acting like they don't even know you.

6. Before you broke up, you guys planned to go to a concert and bought tickets. He:

a. Said he'd still like to go with you, as long as you're still into it.

b. Said he'd still love to go— but with you and a bunch of friends.

c. Asked if one of your friends wanted you to buy his ticket from him.

7. Your birthday was a week after you two broke up. When you saw him in school that day, he:

a. Slipped you a wrapped present he'd bought before the breakup.

b. Smiled, said "Happy birthday," and gave you a hug.

c. Said, "Hey" but didn't mention your birthday at all.

8. You went (uninvited) to his band's gig. When he saw you after the set, he said:

a. "I'm so glad you came. What did you think of those new songs?"

b. "Hey you! Thanks for coming—the more people, the merrier."

c. Nothing—but he did make time to talk to all of his friends . . .

Scoring

Tally your a's, b's, and c's to see if a round two is in your future.

Sara&you
situation
↑

Mostly a's: Instant Replay

Yay! The signs say he still has romantic feeling for you too. If you get back together (and it looks like if you want to, you can), have "The Talk": Discuss what each of you can do differently this time around so you can get beyond the problems that broke you up in the first place.

mostly b's: Bonus Round

He's still into you, but he's not sure about getting back together. So be patient and open to new experiences (and guys), and focus on building a new relationship with him—a friendship. It'll be a good foundation if you two ever decide to take things back to a romantic level.

mostly c's: Game Over

He's moved on, and as much as it hurts, you should too. You can't make him like you, and you need to realize that you deserve a guy who *wants* to be with you, not someone you need to convince! So pick yourself up and get ready to meet a guy who's *really* right for you.

Photo Credits

Front cover: Stephen Lee

Page 3: Stephen Lee

Page 5: Eri Morita

Page 6: Christophe Meimoon

Page 10: Colette DeBarros

Page 11: Colette DeBarros

Page 12: Jan Willem Dikkers

Page 14: Saye

Page 18: Saye

Page 20: Alexie Haye and Justine Parsons

Page 24: Ellen Jong

Page 26: Vincente DiPaulo

Page 30: Saye

Page 32: Jason Todd

Page 36: Ellen Jong

Page 38: Brooke Nipar

Page 40: Saye

Page 46: Saye

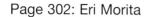

Rock Your Room
with the Hottest Looks!

COSMO **girl** **cool room**
35 **make-it-yourself** projects

Mark Montano

$7.95   978-1-58816-742-2

50 Ways to Get the CosmoGirl Look

COSMO *girl!* Make it Yourself

50 **Fun** and **Funky** Projects

$7.95   978-1-58816-624-1

Fun and Games!

(CG Games: Crosswords)
$5.95   978-1-58816-653-1

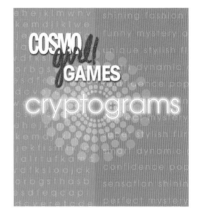

(CG Games: Cryptograms)
$5.95   978-1-58816-711-8

Fun and Games!

(CG Games: Sudoku)
$5.95   978-1-58816-632-6

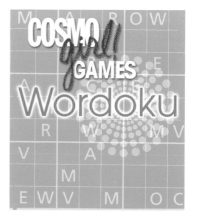

(CG Games: Wordoku)
$5.95   978-1-58816-633-3

Get a Strong and Healthy Body and Mind

COSMOgirl! total body workout
fun moves to look and feel your best

$9.95   978-1-58816-663-0